SELECTED HOMILIES ON FAMILY, LOVE, MARRIAGE, ADULTERY AND DIVORCE

SAINT JOHN CHRYSOSTOM

Translated by
ALEXANDER ROBERTS, JAMES DONALDSON
Edited by
ARTHUR CLEVELAND COXE, PHILIP SCHAFF

SCRIBERE SEMPER ET LEGERE

CONTENTS

1 Cor. vii. 1, 2   1
Ephesians v. 22–24   26
Ephesians vi. 1–3   63
Colossians iv. 12, 13   80
Matt. V. 27, 28.   107

1 COR. VII. 1, 2

(Homily XIX[1])

Now concerning the things whereof ye wrote to
me: it is good for a man not to touch a woman.
But because of fornications, let each man have his
own wife; and let each woman have her own
husband.

Having corrected the three heaviest things
laid to their charge, one, the distraction
of the Church, another, about the fornicator, a third, about the covetous person, he
thenceforth uses a milder sort of speech. And he
interposes some exhortation and advice about
marriage and virginity, giving the hearers some
respite from more unpleasant subjects. But in the

second Epistle he does the contrary; he begins from the milder topics, and ends with the more distressing. And here also, after he has finished his discourse about virginity, he again launches forth into matter more akin to reproof; not setting all down in regular order, but varying his discourse in either kind, as the occasion required and the exigency of the matters in hand.

Wherefore he says, "Now concerning the things whereof ye wrote unto me." For they had written to him, "Whether it was right to abstain from one's wife, or not:" and writing back in answer to this and giving rules about marriage, he introduces also the discourse concerning virginity: "It is good for a man not to touch a woman." "For if," says he, "thou enquire what is the excellent and greatly superior course, it is better not to have any connection whatever with a woman: but if you ask what is safe and helpful to thine own infirmity, be connected by marriage."

But since it was likely, as also happens now, that the husband might be willing but the wife not, or perhaps the reverse, mark how he discusses each case. Some indeed say that this discourse was addressed by him to priests. But I, judging from what follows, could not affirm that it was so: since he would not have given his advice in general terms. For if he were writing these things only for the priests, he would have said, "It is good for the teacher not to touch a woman." But now he has made it of universal application, saying, "It is good for a man;" not for priest only. And again, "Art thou loosed from a wife? Seek not a wife." He said not, "You who are a priest and teacher," but indefinitely. And the whole of his speech goes on entirely in the same tones. And in saying, "Because of fornications, let every man have his own wife" by the very cause alleged for the concession he guides men to continence.

Ver. 3. *"Let the husband pay the wife the honor due to her: in like manner the wife the husband."*

Now what is the meaning of "the due honor? The wife hath not power over her own body;" but is both the slave and the mistress of the husband. And if you decline the service which is due, you have offended God. But if thou wish to withdraw thyself, it must be with the husband's permission, though it be but a for short time. For this is why he calls the matter a debt, to shew that no one is master of himself but that they are servants to each other.

When therefore thou seest an harlot tempting thee, say, "My body is not mine, but my wife's." The same also let the woman say to those who would undermine her chastity, "My body is not mine, but my husband's."

Now if neither husband nor wife hath power even over their own body, much less have they over their property. Hear ye, all that have husbands and all that have wives: that if you must not count your body your own, much less your money.

Elsewhere I grant He gives to the husband abundant precedence, both in the New Testament, and the Old saying, (ἡ ἀποστρόφή σου, LXX. Gen. iii. 16.) "Thy turning shall be towards thy husband, and he shall rule over thee." Paul doth so too by making a distinction thus, and writing, (Ephes. v. 25, 33.) "Husbands, love your wives; and let the wife see that she reverence her husband." But in this place we hear no more of greater and less, but it is one and the same right. Now why is this? Because his speech was about chastity. "In all other things," says he, "let the husband have the prerogative; but not so where the question is about chastity." "The husband hath no power over his own body, neither the wife." There is great equality of honor, and no prerogative.

Ver. 5. "Defraud ye not one the other, except it be by consent."

What then can this mean? "Let not the wife," says he, "exercise continence, if the husband be unwilling; nor yet the husband without the wife's consent." Why so? Because great evils spring from this sort of continence. For adulteries and fornications and the ruin of families have often arisen from hence. For if when men have their own wives they commit fornication, much more if you defraud them of this consolation. And well says he, "Defraud not; fraud" here, and "debt" above, that he might shew the strictness of the right of dominion in question. For that one should practice continence against the will of the other is "defrauding;" but not so, with the other's consent: any more than I count myself defrauded, if after persuading me you take away any thing of mine. Since only he defrauds who takes against another's will and by force. A thing which many women do, working sin rather than righteousness, and thereby becoming accountable for the husband's uncleanness, and rending all asunder. Whereas they should value concord above all things, since this is more important than all beside.

We will, if you please, consider it with a view to actual cases. Thus, suppose a wife and husband, and let the wife be continent, without consent of her husband; well then, if hereupon he commit fornication, or though abstaining from fornication fret and grow restless and be heated and quarrel and give all kind of trouble to his wife; where is all the gain of the fasting and the continence, a breach being made in love? There is none. For what strange reproaches, how much trouble, how great a war must of course arise! since when in an house man and wife are at variance, the house will be no better off than a ship in a storm when the master is upon ill terms with the man at the head. Wherefore he saith, "Defraud not one another, unless it be by consent for a season, that ye may give yourselves unto prayer." It is prayer with unusual earnestness which he here means. For if he is forbidding those who have intercourse with one another to pray, how could "pray without ceasing" have any place? It is possible then to live with a wife and yet give heed unto prayer. But by continence prayer is made more perfect. For he did not say merely, "That ye may pray;" but, "That ye may give yourselves unto it;" as though what he speaks of might cause not uncleanness but much occupation.

"And may be together again, that Satan tempt you not." Thus lest it should seem to be a matter of express enactment, he adds the reason. And what is it? "That Satan tempt you not." And that you may understand that it is not the devil only who causeth this crime, I mean adultery, he adds, "because of your incontinency."

"But this I say by way of permission, not of commandment. For I would that all men were even as I myself; in a state of continence." This he doth in many places when he is advising about difficult matters; he brings forward himself, and says, "Be ye imitators of me."

"Howbeit each man hath his own gift from

God, one after this manner, and another after that." Thus since he had heavily charged them saying, "for your incontinence," he again comforteth them by the words, "each one hath his own gift of God;" not declaring that towards that virtue there is no need of zeal on our part, but, as I was saying before, to comfort them. For if it be a "gift," and man contributes nothing thereunto, how sayest thou, "But (v. 8.) I say to the unmarried and to widows, it is good for them if they abide even as I: (v. 9.) but if they have not continency let them marry?" Do you see the strong sense of Paul how he both signifies that continence is better, and yet puts no force on the person who cannot attain to it; fearing lest some offence arise?

"For it is better to marry than to burn." He indicates how great is the tyranny of concupiscence. What he means is something like this: "If you have to endure much violence and burning desire, withdraw yourself from your pains and toils, lest haply you be subverted."

Ver. 10. "But to the married I give charge, yet not I, but the Lord."

Because it is a law expressly appointed by Christ which he is about to read to them about the "not putting away a wife without fornication; "(S. Matt. v. 32., xix. 9; S. Mark x. 11; S. Luke xvi. 18.) therefore he says, "Not I." True it is what was before spoken though it were not expressly stated, yet it also is His decree. But this, you see, He had delivered in express words. So that the words "I and not I" have this difference of meaning. For that you might not imagine even his own words to be human, therefore he added, "For I think that I also have the Spirit of God."

Now what is that which "to the married the Lord commanded? That the wife depart not from her husband: (v. 11.) but if she depart, let her remain unmarried, or be reconciled unto her husband." Here, seeing that both on the score of continence and other pretexts, and because of infirmities of temper, (μικροψυχίας.) it fell out that separations took place: it were better, he says, that such things should not be at all; but however if they take place, let the wife remain with her husband, if not to cohabit with him, yet so as not to introduce any other to be her husband.

Ver. 12. "But to the rest speak I, not the Lord. If any brother have a wife that believeth not, and she is content to dwell with him, let him not leave her. And if any woman hath an husband that believeth not, and he is content to dwell with her, let her not leave him."

For as when discoursing about separating from fornicators, he made the matter easy by the correction which he applied to his words, saying, "Howbeit, not altogether with the fornicators of this world;" so also in this case he provideth for the abundant easiness of the duty, saying, "If any wife have a husband, or husband a wife, that believeth not, let him not leave her." What sayest thou? "If he be an unbeliever, let him remain with the wife, but not if he be a fornicator? And yet fornication is a less sin than unbelief." I grant, fornication is a less sin: but God spares thine infirmities extremely. And this is what He doth about the sacrifice, saying, (S. Matt. v. 24.) "Leave the sacrifice, and be reconciled to thy brother." This also in the case of the man who owed ten thousand talents. For him too He did not punish for owing him ten thousand talents, but for demanding back a hundred pence from his fellow-servant He took vengeance on him.

Then lest the woman might fear, as though she became unclean because of intercourse with her husband, he says, "For the unbelieving husband is sanctified in the wife, and the unbelieving wife is sanctified in the husband." And yet, if "he that is joined to an harlot is one body," it is quite clear that the woman also who is joined to an idolater is one body. Well: it is one body; nevertheless she becomes not unclean, but the cleanness of the wife overcomes the uncleanness of the husband; and again, the cleanness of the believing husband overcomes the uncleanness of the unbelieving wife.

How then in this case is the uncleanness overcome, and therefore the intercourse allowed; while in the woman who prostitutes herself, the husband is not condemned in casting her out? Because here there is hope that the lost member may be saved through the marriage; but in the other case the marriage has already been dissolved; and there again both are corrupted; but here the fault is in one only of the two. I mean something like this: she that has been guilty of fornication is utterly abominable: if then "he that is joined to an harlot is one body," he also becomes abominable by having connection with an harlot; wherefore all the purity flits away. But in the case before us it is not so. But how? The idolater is unclean but the woman is not unclean. For if indeed she were a partner with him in that wherein he is unclean, I mean his impiety, she herself would also become unclean. But now the idolater is unclean in one way, and the wife holds communion with him in another wherein he is not unclean. For marriage and mixture of bodies is that wherein the communion consists.

Again, there is a hope that this man may be reclaimed by his wife for she is made completely his own: but for the other it is not very easy. For how will she who dishonored him in former times and became another's and destroyed the rights of marriage, have power to reclaim him whom she had wronged; him, moreover, who still remains to her as an alien?

Again in that case, after the fornication the husband is not a husband: but here, although the wife be an idolatress, the husband's rights are not destroyed.

However, he doth not simply recommend co-habitation with the unbeliever, but with the quali-fication that he wills it. Wherefore he said, "And he himself be content to dwell with her." For, tell me, what harm is there when the duties of piety remain unimpaired and there are good hopes about the unbeliever, that those already joined should so abide and not bring in occasions of un-necessary warfare? For the question now is not about those who have never yet come together, but about those who are already joined. He did not say, If any one wish to take an unbelieving wife, but, "If any one hath an unbelieving wife." Which means, If any after marrying or being mar-ried have received the word of godliness, and then the other party which had continued in un-belief still yearn for them to dwell together, let not the marriage be broken off. "For," saith he, "the unbelieving husband is sanctified in the wife." So great is the superabundance of thy purity.

What then, is the Greek holy? Certainly not: for he said not, He is holy; but, "He is sanctified in his wife." And this he said, not to signify that he is holy, but to deliver the woman as completely as possible from her fear and lead the man to desire the truth. For the uncleanness is not in the bodies wherein there is communion, but in the mind and the thoughts. And here follows the proof; namely, that if thou continuing unclean have offspring, the child, not being of thee alone, is of course unclean or half clean. But now it is not unclean. To which effect he adds, "else were your children unclean; but now are they holy;" that is, not unclean. But the Apostle calls them, "holy," by the intensity of the expression again casting out the dread arising from that sort of suspicion.

Ver. 15. "Yet if the unbelieving departeth, let him depart," for in this case the matter is no longer fornication. But what is the meaning of, "if the unbelieving departeth?" For instance, if he bid thee sacrifice and take part in his ungodliness on account of thy marriage, or else part company; it were better the marriage were annulled, and no breach made in godliness. Wherefore he adds, "A brother is not under bondage, nor yet a sister, in such cases." If day by day he buffet thee and keep up combats on this account, it is better to separate. For this is what he glances at, saying, "But God hath called us in peace." For it is the other party who furnished the ground of separation, even as he did who committed uncleanness.

Ver. 16. "For how knowest thou, O wife,

whether thou shalt save thine husband?" This again refers to that expression, "let her not leave him." That is, "if he makes no disturbance, remain," saith he, "for there is even profit in this; remain and advise and give counsel and persuade." For no teacher will have such power to prevail (Reg. πεῖσαι. Bened. ἰσχύσαι.) as a wife. And neither, on one hand, doth he lay any necessity upon her and absolutely demand the point of her, that he may not again do what would be too painful; nor, on the other, doth he tell her to despair: but he leaves the matter in suspense through the uncertainty of the future, saying, "For how knowest thou, O wife, whether thou shalt save thy husband? or how knowest thou, O husband whether thou shalt save thy wife?"

And again, ver. 17. "Only as God hath distributed to each man, as the Lord hath called each, so let him walk. Was any one called being circumcised? let him not become uncircumcised. Was any called in uncircumcision? let him not be circumcised. Circumcision is nothing, and uncircumcision is nothing; but the keeping of the commandments of God. Let each man abide in that calling wherein he was called. Wast thou called, being a slave? Care not for it." These things contribute nothing unto faith, saith he. Be not then contentious neither be troubled; for the faith hath cast out all these things.

"Let each man abide in that calling wherein he was called. Hast thou been called, having an unbelieving wife? Continue to have her. Cast not out thy wife for the faith's sake. Hast thou been called, being a slave? Care not for it. Continue to be a slave. Hast thou been called, being in uncircumcision? Remain uncircumcised. Being circumcised, didst thou become a believer? Continue circumcised. For this is the meaning of, "As God hath distributed unto each man." For these are no hindrances to piety. Thou art called, being a slave; another, with an unbelieving wife; another, being circumcised.

Astonishing! where has he put slavery? As circumcision profits not: and uncircumcision does no harm; so neither doth slavery, nor yet liberty. And that he might point out this with surpassing clearness, he says, "But even (Αλλ' εἰ καὶ δυνάσαι) if thou canst become free, use it rather:" that is, rather continue a slave. Now upon what possible ground does he tell the person who might be set free to remain a slave? He means to point out that slavery is no harm but rather an advantage.

Now we are not ignorant that some say, the words, "use it rather," are spoken with regard to liberty: interpreting it, "if thou canst become free, become free." But the expression would be very contrary to Paul's manner if he intended this. For he would not, when consoling the slave and signifying that he was in no respect injured, have told him to get free. Since perhaps some one might say, "What then, if I am not able? I am an injured and degraded person." This then is not what he says: but as I said, meaning to point out that a man gets nothing by being made free, he says, "Though thou hast it in thy power to be made free, remain rather in slavery."

Next he adds also the cause; "For he that was called in the Lord being a bondservant, is the Lord's free man: likewise he that was called, being free, is Christ's bondservant." "For," saith he, "in the things that relate to Christ, both are equal: and like as thou art the slave of Christ, so also is thy master. How then is the slave a free man? Because He has freed thee not only from sin, but also from outward slavery while continuing a slave. For he suffers not the slave to be a slave, not even though he be a man abiding in slavery: and this is the great wonder.

But how is the slave a free man while continuing a slave? When he is freed from passions and the diseases of the mind: when he looks down upon riches and wrath and all other the like passions.

Ver. 23. "Ye were bought with a price: become not bondservants of men." This saying is addressed not to slaves only but also to free men. For it is possible for one who is a slave not to be a slave; and for one who is a freeman to be a slave. "And how can one be a slave and not a slave?" When he doeth all for God: when he feigns nothing, and doeth nothing out of eye-service towards men: that is how one that is a slave to men can be free. Or again, how doth one that is free become a slave? When he serves men in any evil service, either for gluttony or desire of wealth or for office' sake. For such an one, though he be free, is more of a slave than any man.

And consider both these points. Joseph was a slave but not a slave to men: wherefore even in slavery he was freer than all that are free. For instance, he yielded not to his mistress; yielded not to the purposes which she who possessed him desired. Again she was free; yet none ever so like a slave, courting and beseeching her own servant. But she prevailed not on him, who was free, to do what he would not. This then was not slavery; but it was liberty of the most exalted kind. For what impediment to virtue had he from his slavery? Let men hear, both slaves and free. Which was the slave? He that was entreated or she that did entreat? She that besought or he that despised her supplication?

In fact, there are limits set to slaves by God Himself; and up to what point one ought to keep them, has also been determined, and to transgress them is wrong. Namely, when your master commands nothing which is unpleasing to God, it is right to follow and to obey; but no farther. For thus the slave becomes free. But if you go further, even though you are free you are become a slave. At least he intimates this, saying, "Be not ye the servants of men."

But if this be not the meaning, if he bade them forsake their masters and strive contentiously to become free, in what sense did he exhort them, saying, "Let each one remain in the calling in which he is called?" And in another place, (1 Tim. vi. 1, 2.) "As many servants as are under the yoke, let them count their own masters worthy of all honor; and those that have believing masters, let them not despise them, because they are brethren who partake of the benefit." And writing to the Ephesians also and to the Colossians, he ordains and exacts the same rules. Whence it is plain that it is not this slavery which he annuls, but that which caused as it is by vice befalls free men also: and this is the worst kind of slavery, though he be a free man who is in bondage to it. For what profit had Joseph's brethren of their freedom? Were they not more servile than all slaves; both speaking lies to their father, and to the merchants using false pretences, as well as to their brother? But not such was the free man: rather every where and in all things he was true. And nothing had power to enslave him, neither chain nor bondage nor the love of his mistress nor his being in a strange land. But he abode free every where. For this is liberty in the truest sense when even in bondage it shines through.

Such a thing is Christianity; in slavery it bestows freedom. And as that which is by nature an invulnerable body then shews itself to be invulnerable when having received a dart it suffers no harm; so also he that is strictly free then shows himself, when even under masters he is not enslaved. For this cause his bidding is, "remain a slave." But if it is impossible for one who is a slave to be a Christian such as he ought to be, the Greeks will condemn true religion of great weakness: whereas if they can be taught that slavery in no way impairs godliness, they will admire our doctrine. For if death hurt us not, nor scourges, nor chains, much less slavery. Fire and iron and tyrannies innumerable and diseases and poverty and wild beasts and countless things more dreadful than these, have not been able to injure the faithful; nay, they have made them even mightier. And how shall slavery be able to hurt? It is not slavery itself, beloved, that hurts; but the real slavery is that of sin. And if thou be not a slave in this sense, be bold and rejoice. No one shall have power to do thee any wrong, having the temper which cannot be enslaved. But if thou be a slave to sin, even though thou be ten thousand times free thou hast no good of thy freedom.

For, tell me, what profit is it when, though not in bondage to a man, thou liest down in subjection to thy passions? Since men indeed often know how to spare; but those masters are never satiated with thy destruction. Art thou in bondage to a man? Why, thy master also is slave to thee, in arranging about thy food, in taking care of thy health and in looking after thy shoes and all the other things. And thou dost not fear so much less thou shouldest offend thy master, as he fears lest any of those necessaries should fail thee. "But he sits down, while thou standest." And what of that? Since this may be said of thee as well as of him. Often, at least, when thou art lying down and sleeping sweetly, he is not only standing, but undergoing endless discomforts in the marketplace; and he lies awake more painfully than thou.

For instance; what did Joseph suffer from his mistress to be compared with what she suffered from her evil desire? For he indeed did not the things which she wished to put upon him; but she performed every thing which her mistress ordered her, I mean her spirit of unchastity: which left not off until it had put her to open shame. What master commands such things? what savage tyrant? "Intreat thy slave," that is the word: "flatter the person bought with thy money, supplicate the captive; even if he reject thee with disgust, again besiege him: even if thou speakest to him oftentimes, and he consent not, watch for his being alone, and force him, and become an object of derision." What can be more dishonorable, what more shameful, than these words? "And if even by these means you make no progress, why, accuse him falsely and deceive your husband." Mark how mean, how shameful are the commands, how unmerciful and savage and frantic. What command does the master ever lay on his slave, such as those which her wantonness then laid upon that royal woman? And yet she dare not disobey. But Joseph underwent nothing of this sort, but every thing on the contrary which brought glory and honor.

Would you like to see yet another man under severe orders from a hard mistress, and without spirit to disobey any of them? Consider Cain, what commands were laid on him by his envy. She ordered him to slay his brother, to lie unto God, to grieve his father, to cast off shame; and he did it all, and in nothing refused to obey. And why marvel that over a single person so great should be the power of this mistress? She hath often destroyed entire nations. For instance, the Midianitish women took the Jews, and all but bound them in captivity; their own beauty kindling desire, was the means of their vanquishing that whole nation. Paul then to cast out this sort of slavery, said, "Become not servants of men;" that is, "Obey not men commanding unreasonable things: nay, obey not yourselves." Then having raised up their mind and made it mount on high, he says,

Ver. 25. "Now concerning virgins. I have no commandment of the Lord; but I give my judgment, as one that hath obtained mercy of the Lord to be faithful."

Advancing on his way in regular order, he proceeds next to speak concerning virginity. For after that he had exercised and trained them, in his words concerning continence, he goes forth towards what is greater, saying, "I have no commandment, but I esteem it to be good." For what reason? For the self-same reason as he had mentioned respecting continence.

Ver. 27. "Art thou bound unto a wife? Seek not to be loosed. Art thou loosed from a wife? Seek not a wife."

These words carry no contradiction to what had been said before but rather the most entire agreement with them. For he says in that place also, "Except it be by consent:" as here he says, "Art thou bound unto a wife? Seek not separation." This is no contradiction. For its being against consent makes a dissolution: but if with consent both live continently, it is no dissolution.

Then, lest this should seem to be laying down a law, he subjoins, (v. 28.) "but if thou marry, thou hast not sinned." He next alleges the existing state of things, "the present distress, the shortness of the time," and "the affliction." For marriage draws along with it many things, which indeed he hath glanced at, as well here as also in the discourse about continence: there, by saying, "the wife hath not power over herself;" and here, by the expression, "Thou art bound."

"But if and thou marry, thou hast not sinned." He is not speaking about her who hath made choice of virginity, for if it comes to that, she hath sinned. Since if the widows are condemned for having to do with second marriages after they have once chosen widowhood, much more the virgins.

"But such shall have trouble in the flesh." "And pleasure too," you will say: but observe how he curtails this by the shortness of the time, saying, (v. 28.) "the time is shortened;" that is, "we are exhorted to depart now and go forth, but thou art running further in." And yet even although marriage had no troubles, even so we ought to press on towards things to come. But when it hath affliction too, what need to draw on one's self an additional burden. What occasion to take up such a load, when even after taking it you must use it as having it not? For "those even that have wives must be," he saith, "as though they had none."

Then, having interposed something about the future, he brings back his speech to the present. For some of his topics are spiritual; as that, "the one careth about the things which be her husband's, the other about those which be God's." Others relate to this present life; as, "I would have you to be free from cares." But still with all this he leaves it to their own choice: inasmuch as he who after proving what is best goes back to compulsion, seems as if he did not trust his own statements. Wherefore he rather attracts them by concession, and checks them as follows:

Ver. 35. "And this I say for your own profit, not that I may cast a snare upon you, but for that which is seemly, and that ye may attend upon the Lord without distraction. Let the virgins hear that not by that one point is virginity defined; for she that is careful about the things of the world cannot be a virgin, nor seemly. Thus, when he said, "There is difference between a wife and a virgin," he added this as the difference, and that wherein they are distinguished from each other. And laying down the definition of a virgin and her that is not a virgin, he names, not marriage nor continence but leisure from engagements and multiplicity of engagements. For the evil is not in the

cohabitation, but in the impediment to the strictness of life.

Ver. 36. "But if any man think that he behaveth
himself unseemly toward his virgin."

Here he seems to be talking about marriage;
but all that he says relates to virginity; for he al-
lows even a second marriage, saying, "only in the
Lord." Now what means, "in the Lord?" With
chastity, with honor: for this is needed every
where, and must be pursued for else we cannot
see God.

Now if we have passed lightly by what he says
of virginity, let no one accuse us of negligence; for
indeed an entire book hath been composed by us
upon this topic and as we have there with all the
accuracy which we could, gone through every
branch of the subject, we considered it a waste of
words to introduce it again here. Wherefore, referring the hearer to that work as concerns these
things, we will say this one thing here: We must
follow after continence. For, saith he, "follow after
peace, and the sanctification without which no
one shall see the Lord." Therefore that we may be
accounted worthy to see Him, whether we be in
virginity or in the first marriage or the second, let
us follow after this that we may obtain the
kingdom of heaven, through the grace and lovingkindness of our Lord Jesus Christ; to Whom with

the Father and the Holy Spirit, be glory, power, honor, now, henceforth, and for everlasting ages.

Amen.

---

1. Cf. Nicene and Post-Nicene Fathers: Series I / Volume XII : Homilies on First Corinthians / Homily XIX.

EPHESIANS V. 22–24

(Homily XX[1])

Wives, be in subjection unto your own husbands, as unto the Lord. For the husband is the head of the wife, as Christ also is the head of the Church: being Himself the Saviour of the body. But as the Church is subject to Christ, so let the wives also be to their husbands in everything.

A certain wise man, setting down a number of things in the rank of blessings, set down this also in the rank of a blessing, "A wife agreeing with her husband." (Ecclus. xxv. 1.) And elsewhere again he sets it down among blessings, that a woman should dwell in harmony with her husband. (Ecclus. xl. 23.) And indeed from the beginning, God appears to have made special provision for this union; and discoursing of the twain as one, He said thus, "Male and female created He them" (Gen. i. 27.); and again, "There is neither male nor female." (Gal. iii. 28.) For there is no relationship between man and man so close as that between man and wife, if they be joined together as they should be. And therefore a certain blessed man too, when he would express surpassing love, and was mourning for one that was dear to him, and of one soul with him, did not mention father, nor mother, nor child, nor brother, nor friend, but what? "Thy love to me was wonderful," saith he, "passing the love of women." (2 Sam. i. 26.) For indeed, in very deed, this love is more despotic than any despotism: for others indeed may be strong, but this passion is not only strong, but unfading. For there is a certain love deeply seated in our nature, which imperceptibly to ourselves knits together these bodies of ours. Thus even from the very beginning woman sprang from man, and afterwards from man and woman sprang both man and woman. Perceivest thou the close bond and connection? And how that God suffered not a different kind of nature to enter in from without? And mark, how many providential arrangements He made. He permitted the man to marry his own sister; or rather not his sister, but his daughter; nay, nor yet his daughter, but something more than his daughter, even his own flesh. And thus the whole He framed from one beginning, gathering all together, like stones in a building, into one. For neither on the one hand did He form her from without, and this was that the man might not feel towards her as towards an alien; nor again did He confine marriage to her, that she might not, by contracting herself, and making all center in herself, be cut off from the rest. Thus as in the case of plants, they are of all others the best, which have but a single stem, and spread out into a number of branches; (since were all confined to the root alone, all would be to no purpose, whereas again had it a number of roots, the tree would be no longer worthy of admiration;) so, I say, is the case here also. From one, namely Adam, He made the whole race to spring, preventing them by the strongest necessity from being ever torn asunder, or separated; and afterwards, making it more restricted, He no longer allowed sisters and daughters to be wives, lest we should on the other hand contract our love to one point, and thus in another manner be cut off from one another. Hence Christ said, "He which made them from the beginning, made them male and female." (Matt. xix. 4.)

For great evils are hence produced, and great benefits, both to families and to states. For there is nothing which so welds our life together as the love of man and wife. For this many will lay aside even their arms, for this they will give up life itself. And Paul would never without a reason and without an object have spent so much pains on this subject, as when he says here, "Wives, be in subjection unto your own husbands, as unto the Lord." And why so? Because when they are in harmony, the children are well brought up, and the domestics are in good order, and neighbors, and friends, and relations enjoy the fragrance. But if it be otherwise, all is turned upside down, and thrown into confusion. And just as when the generals of an army are at peace one with another, all things are in due subordination, whereas on the other hand, if they are at variance, everything is turned upside down; so, I say, is it also here. Wherefore, saith he, "Wives, be in subjection unto your own husbands, as unto the Lord."

Yet how strange! for how then is it, that it is said elsewhere, "If one bid not farewell both to wife and to husband, he cannot follow me"? (Luke xiv. 26.) For if it is their duty to be in subjection "as unto the Lord," how saith He that they must depart from them for the Lord's sake? Yet their duty indeed it is, their bounden duty. But the word "as" is not necessarily and universally expressive of exact equality. He either means this, "'as' knowing that ye are servants to the Lord"; (which, by the way, is what he says elsewhere, that, even though they do it not for the husband's sake, yet must they primarily for the Lord's sake;) or else he means, "when thou obeyest thy husband, do so as serving the Lord." For if he who resisteth these external authorities, those of governments, I mean, "withstandeth the ordinance of God" (Rom. xiii. 2.), much more does she who submits not herself to her husband. Such was God's will from the beginning.

Let us take as our fundamental position then that the husband occupies the place of the "head," and the wife the place of the "body."

Ver. 23, 24. Then, he proceeds with arguments and says that "the husband is the head of the wife, as Christ also is the head of the Church, being Himself the Saviour of the body. But as the Church is subject to Christ, so let the wives be to their husbands in everything."

Then after saying, "The husband is the head of the wife, as Christ also is of the Church," he further adds, "and He is the Saviour of the body." For indeed the head is the saving health of the body. He had already laid down beforehand for man and wife, the ground and provision of their love, assigning to each their proper place, to the one that of authority and forethought, to the other that of submission. As then "the Church," that is, both husbands and wives, "is subject unto Christ, so also ye wives submit yourselves to your husbands, as unto God."

Ver. 25. "Husbands, love your wives, even as Christ also loved the Church."

Thou hast heard how great the submission; thou hast extolled and marvelled at Paul, how, like an admirable and spiritual man, he welds together our whole life. Thou didst well. But now hear what he also requires at thy hands; for again he employs the same example.

"Husbands," saith he, "love your wives, even as Christ also loved the Church."

Thou hast seen the measure of obedience, hear also the measure of love. Wouldest thou have thy wife obedient unto thee, as the Church is to Christ? Take then thyself the same provident care for her, as Christ takes for the Church. Yea, even if it shall be needful for thee to give thy life for her, yea, and to be cut into pieces ten thousand times, yea, and to endure and undergo any suffering whatever,—refuse it not. Though thou shouldest undergo all this, yet wilt thou not, no, not even then, have done anything like Christ. For thou indeed art doing it for one to whom thou art already knit; but He for one who turned her back on Him and hated Him. In the same way then as He laid at His feet her who turned her back on Him, who hated, and spurned, and disdained Him, not by menaces, nor by violence, nor by terror, nor by anything else of the kind, but by his unwearied affection; so also do thou behave thyself toward thy wife. Yea, though thou see her looking down upon thee, and disdaining, and scorning thee, yet by thy great thoughtfulness for her, by affection, by kindness, thou wilt be able to lay her at thy feet. For there is nothing more powerful to sway than these bonds, and especially for husband and wife. A servant, indeed, one will be able, perhaps, to bind down by fear; nay not even him, for he will soon start away and be gone. But the partner of one's life, the mother of one's children, the foundation of one's every joy, one ought never to chain down by fear and menaces, but with love and good temper. For what sort of union is that, where the wife trembles at her husband? And what sort of pleasure will the husband himself enjoy, if he dwells with his wife as with a slave, and not as with a free-woman? Yea, though thou shouldest suffer anything on her account, do not upbraid her; for neither did Christ do this.

Ver. 26. "And gave Himself up," he says, "for it, that He might sanctify and cleanse it."

So then she was unclean! So then she had blemishes, so then she was unsightly, so then she was worthless! Whatsoever kind of wife thou shalt take, yet shalt thou never take such a bride as the Church, when Christ took her, nor one so far removed from thee as the Church was from

Christ. And yet for all that, He did not abhor her, nor loathe her for her surpassing deformity. Wouldest thou hear her deformity described? Hear what Paul saith, "For ye were once darkness." (Eph. v. 8.) Didst thou see the blackness of her hue? What blacker than darkness? But look again at her boldness, "living," saith he, "in malice and envy." (Tit. iii. 3.) Look again at her impurity; "disobedient, foolish." But what am I saying? She was both foolish, and of an evil tongue; and yet notwithstanding, though so many were her blemishes, yet did He give Himself up for her in her deformity, as for one in the bloom of youth, as for one dearly beloved, as for one of wonderful beauty. And it was in admiration of this that Paul said, "For scarcely for a righteous man will one die (Rom. v. 7.); and again, "in that while we were yet sinners, Christ died for us." (Rom. v. 8.) And though such as this, He took her, He arrayed her in beauty, and washed her, and refused not even this, to give Himself for her.

Ver. 26, 27. "That He might sanctify it having cleansed it," he proceeds, "by the washing of water with the word; that He might present the Church to Himself a glorious Church, not having spot, or wrinkle, or any such thing, but that it should be holy and without blemish."

"By the washing or laver" He washeth her uncleanness. "By the word," saith he. What word?

"In the Name of the Father, and of the Son, and of the Holy Ghost." (Matt. xxviii. 19.) And not simply hath He adorned her, but hath made her "glorious, not having spot, or wrinkle, or any such thing." Let us then also seek after this beauty ourselves, and we shall be able to create it. Seek not thou at thy wife's hand, things which she is not able to possess. Seest thou that the Church had all things at her Lord's hands? By Him was made glorious, by Him was made pure, by Him made without blemish? Turn not thy back on thy wife because of her deformity. Hear the Scripture that saith, "The bee is little among such as fly, but her fruit is the chief of sweet things." (Ecclus. xi. 3.) She is of God's fashioning. Thou reproachest not her, but Him that made her; what can the woman do? Praise her not for her beauty. Praise and hatred and love based on personal beauty belong to unchastened souls. Seek thou for beauty of soul. Imitate the Bridegroom of the Church. Outward beauty is full of conceit and great license, and throws men into jealousy, and the thing often makes thee suspect monstrous things. But has it any pleasure? For the first or second month, perhaps, or at most for the year: but then no longer; the admiration by familiarity wastes away. Meanwhile the evils which arose from the beauty still abide, the pride, the folly, the contemptuousness. Whereas in one who is not such, there is nothing of this kind. But the love having begun on just grounds, still continues ardent, since its object is beauty of soul, and not of body. What better, tell me, than heaven? What better than the stars? Tell me of what body you will, yet is there none so fair. Tell me of what eyes you will, yet are there none so sparkling. When these were created, the very Angels gazed with wonder, and we gaze with wonder now; yet not in the same degree as at first. Such is familiarity; things do not strike us in the same degree. How much more in the case of a wife! And if moreover disease come too, all is at once fled. Let us seek in a wife affectionateness, modest-mindedness, gentleness; these are the characteristics of beauty. But loveliness of person let us not seek, nor upbraid her upon these points, over which she has no power, nay, rather, let us not upbraid at all, (it were rudeness,) nor let us be impatient, nor sullen. Do ye not see how many, after living with beautiful wives, have ended their lives pitiably, and how many, who have lived with those of no great beauty, have run on to extreme old age with great enjoyment. Let us wipe off the "spot" that is within, let us smooth the "wrinkles" that are within, let us do away the "blemishes" that are on the soul. Such is the beauty God requires. Let us make her fair in God's sight, not in our own. Let us not look for wealth, nor for that high-birth which is outward, but for that true nobility which is in the soul. Let no one endure to get rich by a wife; for such riches are base and disgraceful; no, by no means let any one seek to get rich from this source. "For they that desire to be rich, fall into a temptation and a snare, and many foolish and hurtful lusts, and into destruction and perdition." (1 Tim. vi. 9.) Seek not therefore in thy wife abundance of wealth, and thou shalt find everything else go well. Who, tell me, would overlook the most important things, to attend to those which are less so? And yet, alas! this is in every case our feeling. Yes, if we have a son, we concern ourselves not how he may be made virtuous, but how we may get him a rich wife; not how he may be well-mannered, but well-monied: if we follow a business, we enquire not how it may be clear of sin, but how it may bring us in most profit. And everything has become money; and thus is everything corrupted and ruined, because that passion possesses us.

Ver. 28. "Even so ought husbands to love their own wives," saith he, "as their own bodies."

What, again, means this? To how much greater a similitude, and stronger example has he come; and not only so, but also to one how much nearer and clearer, and to a fresh obligation. For that other one was of no very constraining force, for He was Christ, and was God, and gave Himself. He now manages his argument on a different ground, saying, "so ought men"; because the thing is not a favor, but a debt. Then, "as their own bodies." And why?

Ver. 29. "For no man ever hated his own flesh, but nourisheth and cherisheth it."

That is, tends it with exceeding care. And how is she his flesh? Hearken; "This now is bone of my bones," saith Adam, "and flesh of my flesh." (Gen. ii. 23.) For she is made of matter taken from us. And not only so, but also, "they shall be," saith God, "one flesh." (Gen. ii. 24.)

"Even as Christ also the Church." Here he returns to the former example.

Ver. 30. "Because we are members of His body, of His flesh and of His bones."

Ver. 31. "For this cause shall a man leave his father and mother, and shall cleave to his wife, and the twain shall become one flesh."

Behold again a third ground of obligation; for he shows that a man leaving them that begat him, and from whom he was born, is knit to his wife; and that then the one flesh is, father, and mother, and the child, from the substance of the two commingled. For indeed by the commingling of their seeds is the child produced, so that the three are one flesh. Thus then are we in relation to Christ; we become one flesh by participation, and we much more than the child. And why and how so? Because so it has been from the beginning.

Tell me not that such and such things are so. Seest thou not that we have in our own flesh itself many defects? For one man, for instance, is lame, another has his feet distorted, another his hands withered, another some other member weak; and yet nevertheless he does not grieve at it, nor cut it off, but oftentimes prefers it even to the other. Naturally enough; for it is part of himself. As great love as each entertains towards himself, so great he would have us entertain towards a wife. Not because we partake of the same nature; no, this ground of duty towards a wife is far greater than that; it is that there are not two bodies but one; he the head, she the body. And how saith he elsewhere "and the Head of Christ is God"? (1 Cor. xi. 3.) This I too say, that as we are one body, so also are Christ and the Father One. And thus then is the Father also found to be our Head. He sets down two examples, that of the natural body and that of Christ's body. And hence he further adds,

Ver. 32. "This is great mystery: but I speak in regard of Christ and of the Church."

Why does he call it a great mystery? That it was something great and wonderful, the blessed Moses, or rather God, intimated. For the present, however, saith he, I speak regarding Christ, that having left the Father, He came down, and came to the Bride, and became one Spirit. "For he that is joined unto the Lord is one Spirit." (1 Cor. vi. 17.) And well saith he, "it is a great mystery." And then as though he were saying, "But still nevertheless the allegory does not destroy affection," he adds,

Ver. 33. "Nevertheless do ye also severally love each one his own wife even as himself; and let the wife see that she fear her husband."

For indeed, in very deed, a mystery it is, yea, a great mystery, that a man should leave him that gave him being, him that begat him, and that brought him up, and her that travailed with him and had sorrow, those that have bestowed upon him so many and great benefits, those with whom he has been in familiar intercourse, and be joined to one who was never even seen by him and who has nothing in common with him, and should honor her before all others. A mystery it is indeed. And yet are parents not distressed when these events take place, but rather, when they do not take place; and are delighted when their wealth is spent and lavished upon it.—A great mystery indeed! and one that contains some hidden wisdom. Such Moses prophetically showed it to be from the very first; such now also Paul proclaims it, where he saith, "concerning Christ and the Church."

However not for the husband's sake alone it is thus said, but for the wife's sake also, that "he cherish her as his own flesh, as Christ also the Church," and, "that the wife fear her husband." He is no longer setting down the duties of love only, but what? "That she fear her husband." The wife is a second authority; let not her then demand equality, for she is under the head; nor let him despise her as being in subjection, for she is the body; and if the head despise the body, it will itself also perish. But let him bring in love on his part as a counterpoise to obedience on her part. For example, let the hands and the feet, and all the rest of the members be given up for service to the head, but let the head provide for the body, seeing it contains every sense in itself. Nothing can be better than this union.

And yet how can there ever be love, one may say, where there is fear? It will exist there, I say, preëminently. For she that fears and reverences, loves also; and she that loves, fears and reverences him as being the head, and loves him as being a member, since the head itself is a member of the body at large. Hence he places the one in subjection, and the other in authority, that there may be peace; for where there is equal authority there can never be peace; neither where a house is a democracy, nor where all are rulers; but the ruling power must of necessity be one. And this is universally the case with matters referring to the body, inasmuch as when men are spiritual, there will be peace. There were "five thousand souls," and not one of them said, "that aught of the things which he possessed was his own" (Acts iv. 32.), but they were subject one to another; an indication this of wisdom, and of the fear of God. The principle of love, however, he explains; that of fear he does not. And mark, how on that of love he enlarges, stating the arguments relating to Christ and those relating to one's own flesh, the words, "For this cause shall a man leave his father and mother." (Ver. 31.) Whereas upon those drawn from fear he forbears to enlarge. And why so? Because he would rather that this principle prevail, this, namely, of love; for where this exists, everything else follows of course, but where the other exists, not necessarily. For the man who loves his wife, even though she be not a very obedient one, still will bear with everything. So difficult and impracticable is unanimity, where persons are not bound together by that love which is founded in supreme authority; at all events, fear will not necessarily effect this. Accordingly, he dwells the more upon this, which is the strong tie. And the wife though seeming to be the loser in that she was charged to fear, is the gainer, because the principal duty, love, is charged upon the husband. "But what," one may say, "if a wife reverence me not?" Never mind, thou art to love, fulfill thine own duty. For though that which is due from others may not follow, we ought of course to do our duty. This is an example of what I mean. He says, "submitting yourselves one to another in the fear of Christ." And what then if another submit not himself? Still obey thou the law of God. Just so, I say, is it also here. Let the wife at least, though she be not loved, still reverence notwithstanding, that nothing may lie at her door; and let the husband, though his wife reverence him not, still show her love notwithstanding, that he himself be not wanting in any point. For each has received his own.

This then is marriage when it takes place according to Christ, spiritual marriage, and spiritual birth, not of blood, nor of travail, nor of the will of the flesh. Such was the birth of Christ, not of blood, nor of travail. Such also was that of Isaac. Hear how the Scripture saith, "And it ceased to be with Sarah after the manner of women." (Gen. xviii. 11.) Yea, a marriage it is, not of passion, nor of the flesh, but wholly spiritual, the soul being united to God by a union unspeakable, and which He alone knoweth. Therefore he saith, "He that is joined unto the Lord is one spirit." (1 Cor. vi. 17.) Mark how earnestly he endeavors to unite both flesh with flesh, and spirit with spirit. And where are the heretics? Never surely, if marriage were a thing to be condemned, would he have called Christ and the Church a bride and bridegroom;

never would he have brought forward by way of exhortation the words, "A man shall leave his father and his mother"; and again have added, that it was "spoken in regard of Christ and of the Church." For of her it is that the Psalmist also saith, "Hearken, O daughter, and consider, and incline thine ear; forget also thine own people, and thy father's house. So shall the king desire thy beauty." (Ps. xlv. 10, 11.) Therefore also Christ saith, "I came out from the Father, and am come." (John xvi. 28.) But when I say, that He left the Father, imagine not such a thing as happens among men, a change of place; for just in the same way as the word "go forth" is used, not because He literally came forth, but because of His incarnation, so also is the expression, "He left the Father."

Now why did he not say of the wife also, She shall be joined unto her husband? Why, I say, is this? Because he was discoursing concerning love, and was discoursing to the husband. For to her indeed he discourses concerning reverence, and says, "the husband is the head of the wife" (ver. 23.), and again, "Christ is the Head of the Church." Whereas to him he discourses concerning love, and commits to him this province of love, and declares to him that which pertains to love, thus binding him and cementing him to her. For the man that leaves his father for the sake of his wife, and then again, leaves this very wife herself and abandons her, what forbearance can he deserve?

Seest thou not how great a share of honor God would have her enjoy, in that he hath taken thee away from thy father, and hath linked thee to her? What then, a man may say, if our duty is done, and yet she does not follow the example? "Yet if the unbelieving departeth, let him depart; the brother or the sister is not under bondage in such cases." (1 Cor. vii. 15.)

However, when thou hearest of "fear," demand that fear which becomes a free woman, not as though thou wert exacting it of a slave. For she is thine own body; and if thou do this, thou reproachest thyself in dishonoring thine own body. And of what nature is this "fear"? It is the not contradicting, the not rebelling, the not being fond of the preëminence. It is enough that fear be kept within these bounds. But if thou love, as thou art commanded, thou wilt make it yet greater. Or rather it will not be any longer by fear that thou wilt be doing this, but love itself will have its effect. The sex is somehow weaker, and needs much support, much condescension.

But what will they say, who are knit together in second marriages? I speak not at all in condemnation of them, God forbid; for the Apostle himself permits them, though indeed by way of condescension.

Supply her with everything. Do everything and endure trouble for her sake. Necessity is laid upon thee.

Here he does not think it right to introduce his counsel, as he in many cases does, with examples from them that are without. That of Christ, so great and forcible, were alone enough; and more especially as regards the argument of subjection. "A man shall leave," he saith, "his father and mother." Behold, this then is from without. But he does not say, and "shall dwell with," but "shall cleave unto," thus showing the closeness of the union, and the fervent love. Nay, he is not content with this, but further by what he adds, he explains the subjection in such a way as that the twain appear no longer twain. He does not say, "one spirit," he does not say, "one soul" (for that is manifest, and is possible to any one), but so as to be "one flesh." She is a second authority, possessing indeed an authority, and a considerable equality of dignity; but at the same time the husband has somewhat of superiority. In this consists most chiefly the well-being of the house. For he took that former argument, the example of Christ, to show that we ought not only to love, but also to govern; "that she may be," saith he, "holy and without blemish." But the word "flesh" has reference to love—and the word "shall cleave" has in like manner reference to love. For if thou shalt make her "holy and without blemish," everything else will follow. Seek the things which are of God, and those which are of man will follow readily enough. Govern thy wife, and thus will the whole house be in harmony. Hear what Paul saith. "And if they would learn anything, let them ask their own husbands at home." (1 Cor. xiv. 35.) If we thus regulate our own houses, we shall be also fit for the management of the Church. For indeed a house is a little Church. Thus it is possible for us by becoming good husbands and wives, to surpass all others.

Consider Abraham, and Sarah, and Isaac, and the three hundred and eighteen born in his house. (Gen. xiv. 14.) How the whole house was harmoniously knit together, how the whole was full of piety and fulfilled the Apostolic injunction. She also "reverenced her husband"; for hear her own words, "It hath not yet happened unto me even until now, and my lord is old also." (Gen. xviii. 12.) And he again so loved her, that in all things he obeyed her commands. And the young child was virtuous, and the servants born in the house, they too were so excellent that they refused not even to hazard their lives with their master; they delayed not, nor asked the reason. Nay, one of them, the chief, was so admirable, that he was even entrusted with the marriage of the only-begotten child, and with a journey into a foreign country. (Gen. xxiv. 1–67.) For just as with a general, when his soldiery also is well organized, the enemy has no quarter to attack; so, I say, is it also here: when husband and wife and children and servants are all interested in the same things, great is the harmony of the house. Since where this is not the case, the whole is oftentimes overthrown and broken up by one bad servant; and that single one will often mar and utterly destroy the whole.

Moral. Let us then be very thoughtful both for our wives, and children, and servants; knowing that we shall thus be establishing for ourselves an easy government, and shall have our accounts with them gentle and lenient, and say, "Behold I, and the children which God hath given me." (Isa. viii. 18.) If the husband command respect, and the head be honorable, then will the rest of the body sustain no violence. Now what is the wife's fitting behavior, and what the husband's, he states accurately, charging her to reverence him as the head, and him to love her as a wife; but how, it may be said, can these things be? That they ought indeed so to be, he has proved. But how they can be so, I will tell you. They will be so, if we will despise money, if we will look but to one thing only, excellence of soul, if we will keep the fear of God before our eyes. For what he says in his discourse to servants, "whatsoever any man doeth, whether it be good or evil, the same shall he receive of the

Lord" (Eph. vi. 8.); this is also the case here. Love her therefore not for her sake so much as for Christ's sake. This, at least, he as much as intimates, in saying, "as unto the Lord." So then do everything, as in obedience to the Lord, and as doing everything for His sake. This were enough to induce and to persuade us, and not to suffer that there should be any teasing and dissension. Let none be believed when slandering the husband to his wife; no, nor let the husband believe anything at random against the wife, nor let the wife be without reason inquisitive about his goings out and his comings in. No, nor on any account let the husband ever render himself worthy of any suspicion whatever. For what, tell me, what if thou shalt devote thyself all the day to thy friends, and give the evening to thy wife, and not even thus be able to content her, and place her out of reach of suspicion? Though thy wife complain, yet be not annoyed—it is her love, not her folly— they are the complaints of fervent attachment, and burning affection, and fear. Yes, she is afraid lest any one have stolen her marriage bed, lest any one have injured her in that which is the summit of her blessings, lest any one have taken away from her him who is her head, lest any one have broken through her marriage chamber.

There is also another ground of petty jealousy. Let neither claim too much service of the servants, neither the husband from the maid-servant, nor the wife from the man-servant. For these things also are enough to beget suspicion. For consider, I say, that righteous household I spoke of. Sarah herself bade the patriarch take Hagar. She herself directed it, no one compelled her, nor did the husband attempt it; no, although he had dragged on so long a period childless, yet he chose never to become a father, rather than to grieve his wife. And yet even after all this, what said Sarah? "The Lord judge between me and thee." (Gen. xvi. 5.) Now, I say, had he been any one else would he not have been moved to anger? Would he not also have stretched forth his hand, saying as it were, "What meanest thou? I had no desire to have anything to do with the woman; it was all thine own doing; and dost thou turn again and accuse me?" —But no, he says nothing of the sort;—but what? "Behold, thy maid is in thy hand; do to her that which is good in thine eyes." (Gen. xvi. 6.) He delivered up the partner of his bed, that he might not grieve Sarah. And yet surely is there nothing greater than this for producing affection. For if partaking of the same table produces unanimity even in robbers towards their foes, (and the Psalmist saith, "Who didst eat sweet food at the same table with me"); much more will the becoming one flesh—for such is the being the partner of the bed—be effectual to draw us together. Yet did none of these things avail to overcome him; but he delivered Hagar up to his wife, to show that nothing had been done by his own fault. Nay, and what is more, he sent her forth when with child. Who would not have pitied one that had conceived a child by himself? Yet was the just man unmoved, for he set before everything else the love he owed his wife.

Let us then imitate him ourselves. Let no one reproach his neighbor with his poverty; let no one be in love with money; and then all difficulties will be at an end.

Neither let a wife say to her husband, "Unmanly coward that thou art, full of sluggishness and dullness, and fast asleep! here is such a one, a low man, and of low parentage, who runs his risks, and makes his voyages, and has made a good fortune; and his wife wears her jewels, and goes out with her pair of milk-white mules; she rides about everywhere, she has troops of slaves, and a swarm of eunuchs, but thou hast cowered down and livest to no purpose." Let not a wife say these things, nor anything like them. For she is the body, not to dictate to the head, but to submit herself and obey. "But how," some one will say, "is she to endure poverty? Where is she to look for consolation?" Let her select and put beside her those who are poorer still. Let her again consider how many noble and high-born maidens have not only received nothing of their husbands, but have even given dowries to them, and have spent their all upon them. Let her reflect on the perils which arise from such riches, and she will cling to this quiet life. In short, if she is affectionately disposed towards her husband, she will utter nothing of the sort. No, she will rather choose to have him near her, though gaining nothing, than gaining ten thousand talents of gold, accompanied with that care and anxiety which always arise to wives from those distant voyages.

Neither, however, let the husband, when he hears these things, on the score of his having the supreme authority, betake himself to revilings and to blows; but let him exhort, let him admonish her, as being less perfect, let him persuade her with arguments. Let him never once lift his hand, —far be this from a noble spirit,—no, nor give expression to insults, or taunts, or revilings; but let him regulate and direct her as being wanting in wisdom. Yet how shall this be done? If she be instructed in the true riches, in the heavenly philosophy, she will make no complaints like these. Let him teach her then, that poverty is no evil. Let him teach her, not by what he says only, but also by what he does. Let him teach her to despise glory; and then his wife will speak of nothing, and will desire nothing of the kind. Let him, as if he had an image given into his hands to mould, let him, from that very evening on which he first receives her into the bridal chamber, teach her temperance, gentleness, and how to live, casting down the love of money at once from the outset, and from the very threshold. Let him discipline her in wisdom, and advise her never to have bits of gold hanging at her ears, and down her cheeks, and laid round about her neck, nor laid up about the chamber, nor golden and costly garments stored up. But let her chamber be handsome, still let not what is handsome degenerate into finery. No, leave these things to the people of the stage. Adorn thine house thyself with all possible neatness, so as rather to breathe an air of soberness than much perfume. For hence will arise two or three good results. First then, the bride will not be grieved, when the apartments are opened, and the tissues, and the golden ornaments, and silver vessels, are sent back to their several owners. Next, the bridegroom will have no anxiety about the loss, nor for the security of the accumulated treasures. Thirdly again, in addition to this, which is the crown of all these benefits, by these very points he will be showing his own judgment, that indeed he has no pleasure in any of these things, and that he will moreover put an end to everything else in keeping with them, and will never so much as allow the existence either of dances, or of immodest songs. I am aware that I shall appear perhaps ridiculous to many persons, in giving such admonitions. Still nevertheless, if ye will but listen to me, as time goes on, and the benefit of the practice accrues to you, then ye will understand the advantage of it. And the laughter will pass off, and ye will laugh at the present fashion, and will see that the present practice is really that of silly children and of drunken men. Whereas what I recommend is the part of soberness, and wisdom, and of the sublimest way of life. What then do I say is our duty? Take away from marriage all those shameful, those Satanic, those immodest songs, those companies of profligate young people, and this will avail to chasten the spirit of thy bride. For she will at once thus reason with herself; "Wonderful! What a philosopher this man is! he regards the present life as nothing, he has brought me here into his house, to be a mother, to bring up his children, to manage his household affairs." "Yes, but these things are distasteful to a bride?" Just for the first or second day;—but not afterwards; nay, she will even reap from them the greatest delight, and relieve herself of all suspicion. For a man who can endure neither flute-players, nor dancers, nor broken songs, and that too at the very time of his wedding, that man will scarcely endure ever to do or say anything shameful. And then after this, when thou hast stripped the marriage of all these things, then take her, and form and mould her carefully, encouraging her bashfulness to a considerable length of time, and not destroying it suddenly. For even if the damsel be very bold, yet for a time she will keep silence out of reverence for her husband, and feeling herself a novice in the circumstances. Thou then break not off this reserve too hastily, as unchaste husbands do, but encourage it for a long time. For this will be a great advantage to thee. Meanwhile she will not complain, she will not find fault with any laws thou mayest frame for her. During that time therefore, during which shame, like a sort of bridle laid upon the soul, suffers her not to make any murmur, nor to complain of what is done, lay down all thy laws. For as soon as ever she acquires boldness, she will overturn and confound everything without any sense of fear. When is there then another time so advantageous for moulding a wife, as that during which she reverences her husband, and is still timid, and still shy? Then lay down all thy laws for her, and willing or unwilling, she will certainly obey them. But how shalt thou help spoiling her modesty? By showing her that thou thyself art no less modest than she is, addressing to her but few words, and those too with great gravity and collectedness. Then entrust her with the discourses of wisdom, for her soul will receive them. And establish her in that loveliest habit, I mean modesty. If you wish me, I will also tell you by way of specimen, what sort of language should be addressed to her. For if Paul shrank not from saying, "Defraud ye not one the other" (2 Cor. vii. 5.), and spoke the language of a bridesmaid, or rather not of a bridesmaid, but of a spiritual soul, much more will not we shrink from speaking. What then is the language we ought to address to her? With great delicacy then we may say to her, "I have taken thee, my child, to be partner of my life, and have brought thee in to share with me in the closest and most honorable ties, in my children, and the superintendence of my house. And what advice then shall I now rec-ommend thee?" But rather, first talk with her of your love for her; for there is nothing that so con-tributes to persuade a hearer to admit sincerely the things that are said, as to be assured that they are said with hearty affection. How then art thou to show that affection? By saying, "when it was in my power to take many to wife, both with better fortunes, and of noble family, I did not so choose, but I was enamoured of thee, and thy beautiful life, thy modesty, thy gentleness, and soberness of mind." Then immediately from these beginnings open the way to your discourse on true wisdom, and with some circumlocution make a protest against riches. For if you direct your argument at once against riches, you will bear too heavily upon her; but if you do it by taking an occasion, you will succeed entirely. For you will appear to be doing it in the way of an apology, not as a morose sort of person, and ungracious, and over-nice about trifles. But when you take occasion from what relates to herself, she will be even pleased. You will say then, (for I must now take up the discourse again,) that "whereas I might have married a rich woman, and with good fortune, I could not endure it. And why so? Not capriciously, and without reason; but I was taught well and truly, that money is no real possession, but a most despicable thing, a thing which moreover belongs as well to thieves, and to harlots, and to grave-robbers. So I gave up these things, and went on till I fell in with the excellence of thy soul, which I value above all gold. For a young damsel who is discreet and ingenuous, and whose heart is set on piety, is worth the whole world. For these reasons then, I courted thee, and I love thee, and prefer thee to my own soul. For the present life is nothing. And I pray, and beseech, and do all I can, that we may be counted worthy so to live this present life, as that we may be able also there in the world to come to be united to one another in perfect security. For our time here is brief and fleeting. But if we shall be counted worthy by having pleased God to so exchange this life for that one, then shall we ever be both with Christ and with each other, with more abundant pleasure. I value thy affection above all things, and nothing is so bitter or so painful to me, as ever to be at variance with thee. Yes, though it should be my lot to lose my all, and to become poorer than Irus, and undergo the extremest hazards, and suffer any pain whatsoever, all will be tolerable and endurable, so long as thy feelings are true towards me. And then will my children be most dear to me, whilst thou art affectionately disposed towards me. But thou must do these duties too." Then mingle also with your discourse the Apostle's words, that "thus God would have our affections blended together; for listen to the Scripture, which saith, 'For this cause shall a man leave his father and mother, and cleave to his wife.' Let us have no pretext for narrow-minded jealousy. Perish riches, and retinue of slaves, and all your outward pomps. To me this is more valuable than all." What weight of gold, what amount of treasures, are so dear to a wife as these words? Never fear that because she is beloved she will ever rave against thee, but confess that thou lovest her. For courtezans indeed, who now attach themselves to one and now to another, would naturally enough feel contempt towards their lovers, should they hear such expressions as these; but a freeborn wife or a noble damsel would never be so affected with such words; no, she will be so much the more subdued. Show her too, that you set a high value on her company, and that you are more desirous to be at home for her sake, than in the market-place. And esteem her before all your friends, and above the children that are born of her, and let these very children be beloved by thee for her sake. If she does any good act, praise and admire it; if any foolish one, and such as girls may chance to do, advise her and remind her. Condemn out and out all riches and extravagance, and gently point out the ornament that there is in neatness and in modesty; and be continually teaching her the things that are profitable.

Let your prayers be common. Let each go to Church; and let the husband ask his wife at home, and she again ask her husband, the account of the things which were said and read there. If any poverty should overtake you, cite the case of those holy men, Paul and Peter, who were more honored than any kings or rich men; and yet how they spent their lives, in hunger and in thirst. Teach her that there is nothing in life that is to be feared, save only offending against God. If any marry thus, with these views, he will be but little inferior to monks; the married but little below the unmarried.

If thou hast a mind to give dinners, and to make entertainments, let there be nothing immodest, nothing disorderly. If thou shouldest find any poor saint able to bless your house, able only just by setting his foot in it to bring in the whole blessing of God, invite him. And shalt I say more-over another thing? Let no one of you make it his endeavor to marry a rich woman, but much rather a poor one. When she comes in, she will not bring so great a source of pleasure from her riches, as she will annoyance from her taunts, from her demanding more than she brought, from her insolence, her extravagance, her vexatious language. For she will say perhaps, "I have not yet spent anything of thine, I am still wearing my own apparel, bought with what my parents set-tled upon me." What sayest thou, O woman? Still wearing thine own! And what can be more miser-able than this language? Why, thou hast no longer a body of thine own, and hast thou money of thine own? After marriage ye are no longer twain, but are become one flesh, and are then your pos-sessions twain, and not one? Oh! this love of money! Ye both are become one man, one living creature; and dost thou still say "mine own"? Cursed and abominable word that it is, it was brought in by the devil. Things far nearer and dearer to us than these hath God made all common to us, and are these then not common? We cannot say, "my own light, my own sun, my own water": all our greater blessings are com-mon, and are riches not common? Perish the riches ten thousand times over! Or rather not the riches, but those tempers of mind which know not how to make use of riches, but esteem them above all things.

Teach her these lessons also with the rest, but with much graciousness. For since the recommendation of virtue has in itself much that is stern, and especially to a young and tender damsel, whenever discourses on true wisdom are to be made, contrive that your manner be full of grace and kindness. And above all banish this notion from her soul, of "mine and thine." If she say the word "mine," say unto her, "What things dost thou call thine? For in truth I know not; I for my part have nothing of mine own. How then speakest thou of 'mine,' when all things are thine?" Freely grant her the word. Dost thou not perceive that such is our practice with children? When, whilst we are holding anything, a child snatches it, and wishes again to get hold of some other thing, we allow it, and say, "Yes, and this is thine, and that is thine." The same also let us do with a wife; for her temper is more or less like a child's; and if she says "mine," say, "why, everything is thine, and I am thine." Nor is the expression one of flattery, but of exceeding wisdom. Thus wilt thou be able to abate her wrath, and put an end to her disappointment. For it is flattery when a man does an unworthy act with an evil object: whereas this is the highest philosophy. Say then, "Even I am thine, my child; this advice Paul gives me where he says, 'The husband hath not power over his own body, but the wife.' (1 Cor. vii. 4.) If I have no power over my body, but thou hast, much more hast thou over my possessions." By saying these things thou wilt have quieted her, thou wilt have quenched the fire, thou wilt have shamed the devil, thou wilt have made her more thy slave than one bought with money, with this language thou wilt have bound her fast. Thus then, by thine own language, teach her never to speak of "mine and thine." And again, never call her simply by her name, but with terms of endearment, with honor, with much love. Honor her, and she will not need honor from others; she will not want the glory that comes from others, if she enjoys that which comes from thee. Prefer her before all, on every account, both for her beauty and her discernment, and praise her. Thou wilt thus persuade her to give heed to none that are without, but to scorn all the world except thyself. Teach her the fear of God, and all good things will flow from this as from a fountain, and the house will be full of ten thousand blessings. If we seek the things that are incorruptible, these corruptible things will follow. "For," saith He, "seek first His kingdom, and all these things shall be added unto you." (Matt. vi. 33.) What sort of persons, think you, must the children of such parents be? What the servants of such masters? What all others who come near them? Will not they too eventually be loaded with blessings out of number? For generally the servants also have their characters formed after their master's, and are fashioned after their humors, love the same objects, which they have been taught to love, speak the same language, and engage with them in the same pursuits. If thus we regulate ourselves, and attentively study the Scriptures, in most things we shall derive instruction from them. And thus shall be able to please God, and to pass through the whole of the present life virtuously, and to attain those blessings which are promised to those that love Him, of which God grant that we may all be counted worthy, through the grace and lovingkindness of our Lord Jesus Christ, with Whom, together with the Holy Ghost, be unto the Father, glory, power, and honor, now, and ever, through all ages.

Amen.

---

1. Cf. Nicene and Post-Nicene Fathers: Series I, Volume XIII: Homilies on Galatians, Ephesians, Philippians, Colossians, Thessalonians, Timothy, Titus, and Philemon / On Ephesians / Homily XX.

EPHESIANS VI. 1–3

(Homily XXI[1])

Children, obey your parents in the Lord, for this is
right. Honor thy father and mother (which is the
first commandment with promise), that it may be
well with thee, and thou mayest live long on the
earth.

As a man in forming a body, places the
head first, after that the neck, then the
feet, so does the blessed Paul proceed in
his discourse. He has spoken of the husband, he
has spoken of the wife, who is second in authority,
he now goes on by gradual advances to the third
rank—which is that of children. For the husband
has authority over the wife, and the husband and

the wife over the children. Now then mark what
he is saying.

"Children, obey your parents in the Lord; for
this is the first commandment with promise."

Here he has not a word of discourse concerning Christ, not a word on high subjects, for he
is as yet addressing his discourse to tender under-
standings. And it is for this reason, moreover, that
he makes his exhortation short, inasmuch as children cannot follow up a long argument. For this
reason also he does not discourse at all about a
kingdom, (because it does not belong to the
tender age of childhood to understand these subjects,) but what a child's soul most especially
longs to hear, that he says, namely, that it shall
"live long." For if any one shall enquire why it is
that he omitted to discourse concerning a kingdom, but set before them the commandment laid
down in the law, he does this because he speaks to
them as infantile, and because he is well aware
that if the husband and the wife are thus disposed
according to the law which he has laid down,
there will be but little trouble in securing the submission of the children. For whenever any matter
has a good and sound and orderly principle and
foundation, everything will thenceforward go on
with method and regularity, with much facility:
the more difficult thing is to settle the foundation,
to lay down a firm basis. "Children," saith he,

"obey your parents in the Lord," that is, according to the Lord. This, he means to say, is what God commands you. But what then if they shall command foolish things? Generally a father, however foolish he may be himself, does not command foolish things. However, even in that case, the Apostle has guarded the matter, by saying, "in the Lord"; that is, wherever you will not be offending against God. So that if the father be a gentile or a heretic, we ought no longer to obey, because the command is not then, "in the Lord." But how is it that he says, "Which is the first commandment"? For the first is, "Thou shalt not commit adultery; —Thou shalt not kill." He does not speak of it then as first in rank, but in respect of the promise. For upon those others there is no reward annexed, as being enacted with reference to evil things, and to departure from evil things. Whereas in these others, where there is the practice of good, there is further a promise held out. And observe how admirable a foundation he has laid for the path of virtue, that is, honor and reverence towards parents. When he would lead us away from wicked practices, and is just about to enter upon virtuous ones, this is the first thing he enjoins, honor towards parents; inasmuch as they before all others are, after God, the authors of our being, so that it is reasonable they should be the first to reap the fruits of our right actions; and then all the rest of mankind. For if a man have not this honor for parents he will never be gentle toward those unconnected with him.

However, having given the necessary injunctions to children, he passes to the fathers, and says,

Ver. 4. "And ye fathers, provoke not your children to wrath; but nurture them up in the chastening and admonition of the Lord."

He does not say, "love them," because to this nature draws them even against their own will, and it were superfluous to lay down a law on such subjects. But what does he say? "Provoke not your children to wrath," as many do by disinheriting them, and disowning them, and treating them overbearingly, not as free, but as slaves. This is why he says, "Provoke not your children to wrath." Then, which is the chief thing of all, he shows how they will be led to obedience, referring the whole source of it to the head and chief authority. And in the same way as he has shown the husband to be the cause of the wife's obedience, (which is the reason also why he addresses the greater part of his arguments to him, advising him to attach her to himself by the power of love,) so, I say, here also, he refers the efficiency to him, by saying, "But bring them up in the chastening and admonition of the Lord." Thou seest that where there are spiritual ties, the natural ties will follow.

Do you wish your son to be obedient? From the very first "Bring him up in the chastening and admonition of the Lord." Never deem it an unnecessary thing that he should be a diligent hearer of the divine Scriptures. For there the first thing he hears will be this, "Honor thy father and thy mother"; so that this makes for thee. Never say, this is the business of monks. Am I making a monk of him? No. There is no need he should become a monk. Why be so afraid of a thing so replete with so much advantage? Make him a Christian. For it is of all things necessary for laymen to be acquainted with the lessons derived from this source; but especially for children. For theirs is an age full of folly; and to this folly are superadded the bad examples derived from the heathen tales, where they are made acquainted with those heroes so admired amongst them, slaves of their passions, and cowards with regard to death; as, for example, Achilles, when he relents, when he dies for his concubine, when another gets drunk, and many other things of the sort. He requires therefore the remedies against these things. How is it not absurd to send children out to trades, and to school, and to do all you can for these objects, and yet, not to "bring them up in the chastening and admonition of the Lord"? And for this reason truly we are the first to reap the fruits, because we bring up our children to be insolent and profligate, disobedient, and mere vulgar fellows. Let us not then do this; no, let us listen to this blessed Apostle's admonition. "Let us bring them up in the chastening and admonition of the Lord." Let us give them a pattern. Let us make them from the earliest age apply themselves to the reading of the Scriptures. Alas, that so constantly as I repeat this, I am looked upon as trifling! Still, I shall not cease to do my duty. Why, tell me, do ye not imitate them of old? Ye women, especially, emulate those admirable women. Has a child been born to any one? Imitate Hannah's example (1 Sam. i. 24.); look at what she did. She brought him up at once to the temple. Who amongst you would not rather that his son should become a Samuel than that he should be king of the whole world ten thousand times over? "And how," you will say, "is it possible he should become such a one?" Why is it not possible? It is because thou dost not choose it thyself, nor committest him to the care of those who are able to make him such a one. "And who," it will be said, "is such a one as this?" God. Since she put him into the hands of God. For not even Eli himself was one of those in any great degree qualified to form him; (how could he be, he who was not able to form even his own children?) No, it was the faith of the mother and her earnest zeal that wrought the whole. He was her first child, and her only one, and she knew not whether she should ever have others besides. Yet she did not say, "I will wait till the child is grown up, that he may have a taste of the things of this life, I will allow him to have his pastime in them a little in his childish years." No, all these thoughts the woman repudiated, she was absorbed in one object, how from the very beginning she might dedicate the spiritual image to God. Well may we men be put to the blush at the wisdom of this woman. She offered him up to God, and there she left him. And therefore was her married state more glorious, in that she had made spiritual objects her first care, in that she dedicated the first-fruits to God. Therefore was her womb fruitful, and she obtained other children besides. And therefore she saw him honorable even in the world. For if men when they are honored, render honor in return, will not God much more, He who does this, even without being honored? How long are we to be mere lumps of flesh? How long are we to be stooping to the earth? Let everything be secondary with us to the provident care we should take of our children, and to our "bringing them up in the chastening and admonition of the Lord." If from the very first he is taught to be a lover of true wisdom, then wealth greater than all wealth has he acquired and a more imposing name. You will effect nothing so great by teaching him an art, and giving him that outward learning by which he will gain riches, as if you teach him the art of despising riches. If you desire to make him rich, do this. For the rich man is not he who desires great riches, and is encircled with great riches; but the man who has need of nothing. Discipline your son in this, teach him this. This is the greatest riches. Seek not how to give him reputation and high character in outward learning, but consider deeply how you shall teach him to despise the glory that belongs to this present life. By this means would he become more distinguished and more truly glorious. This it is possible for the poor man and the rich man alike to accomplish. These are lessons which a man does not learn from a master, nor by art, but by means of the divine oracles. Seek not how he shall enjoy a long life here, but how he shall enjoy a boundless and endless life hereafter. Give him the great things, not the little things. Hear what Paul saith, "Bring them up in the chastening and admonition of the Lord"; study not to make him an orator, but train him up to be a philosopher. In the want of the one there will be no harm whatever; in the absence of the other, all the rhetoric in the world will be of no advantage. Tempers are wanted, not talking; character, not cleverness; deeds, not words. These gain a man the kingdom. These confer what are benefits indeed. Whet not his tongue, but cleanse his soul. I do not say this to prevent your teaching him these things, but to prevent your attending to them exclusively. Do not imagine that the monk alone stands in need of these lessons from Scripture. Of all others, the children just about to enter into the world specially need them. For just in the same way as the man who is always at anchor in harbor, is not the man who requires his ship to be fitted out and who needs a pilot and a crew, but he who is always out at sea; so is it with the man of the world and the monk. The one is entered as it were into a waveless harbor, and lives an untroubled life, and far removed from every storm; whilst the other is ever on the ocean, and lives out at sea in the very midst of the ocean, battling with billows without number.

And though he may not need it himself, still he ought to be so prepared as to stop the mouths of others. Thus the more distinguished he is in the present life, so much the more he stands in need of this education. If he passes his life in courts, there are many Heathens, and philosophers, and persons puffed up with the glory of this life. It is like a place full of dropsical people. Such in some sort is the court. All are, as it were, puffed up, and in a state of inflammation. And they who are not so are studying to become so. Now then reflect how vast a benefit it is, that your son on entering there, should enter like an excellent physician, furnished with instruments which may allay every one's peculiar inflammation, and should go up to every one, and converse with him, and restore the diseased body to health, applying the remedies derived from the Scriptures, and pouring forth discourses of the true philosophy. For with whom is the recluse to converse? with his wall and his ceiling? yea, or again with the wilderness and the woods? or with the birds and the trees? He therefore has not so great need of this sort of discipline. Still, however, he makes it his business to perfect this work, not so much with a view of disciplining others as himself. There is then every need of much discipline of this sort to those that are to mix in the present world, because such an one has a stronger temptation to sin than the other. And if you have a mind to understand it, he will further be a more useful person even in the world itself. For all will have a reverence for him from these words, when they see him in the fire without being burnt, and not desirous of power. But power he will then obtain, when he least desires it, and will be a still higher object of respect to the king; for it is not possible that such a character should be hid. Amongst a number of healthy persons, indeed, a healthy man will not be noticed; but when there is one healthy man amongst a number of sick, the report will quickly spread and reach the king's ears, and he will make him ruler over many nations. Knowing then these things, "bring up your children in the chastening and admonition of the Lord."

"But suppose a man is poor." Still he will be in no wise more insignificant than the man who lives in kings' courts, because he is not in kings' courts; no, he will be held in admiration, and will soon gain that authority which is yielded voluntarily, and not by any compulsion. For if a set of Greeks, men worthless as they are, and dogs, by taking up that worthless philosophy of theirs, (for such the Grecian philosophy is,) or rather not itself but only its mere name, and wearing the threadbare cloak, and letting their hair grow, impress many; how much more will he who is a true philosopher? If a false appearance, if a mere shadow of philosophy at first sight so catches us, what if we should love the true and pure philosophy? Will not all court it, and entrust both houses, and wives, and children, with full confidence to such men? But there is not, no, there is not such a philosopher existing now. And therefore, it is not possible to find an example of the sort. Amongst recluses, indeed, there are such, but amongst people in the world no longer. And that amongst recluses there are such, it would be possible to adduce a number of instances. However, I will mention one out of many. Ye know, doubtless, and have heard of, and some, perhaps, have also seen, the man whom I am now about to mention. I mean, the admirable Julian. This man was a rustic, in humble life, and of humble parentage, and totally uninstructed in all outward accomplishments, but full of unadorned wisdom. When he came into the cities, (and this was but rarely,) never did such a concourse take place, not when orators, or sophists, or any one else rode in. But what am I saying? Is not his very name more glorious than that of any king's, and celebrated even to this day? And if these things were in this world, in the world in which the Lord promised us no one good thing, in which He hath told us we are strangers, let us consider how great will be the blessings laid up for us in the heavens. If, where they were sojourners they enjoyed so great honor, how great glory shall they enjoy where their own city is! If, where He promised tribulation, they meet with such attentive care, then where He promises true honors, how great shall be their rest!

And now would ye have me exhibit examples of secular men? At present, indeed, we have none; still there are perhaps even secular men who are excellent, though not arrived at the highest philosophy. I shall therefore quote you examples from the saints of the ancient times. How many, who had wives to keep and children to bring up, were inferior in no respect, no, in no respect to those who have been mentioned? Now, however, it is no longer so, "by reason of the present distress" (1 Cor. vii. 26.), as this blessed Apostle saith. Now then whom would ye have me mention? Noah, or Abraham? The son of the one or of the other? Or again, Joseph? Or would ye have me go to the Prophets? Moses I mean, or Isaiah? However, if you will, let us carry our discourse to Abraham, whom all are continually bringing forward to us above all others. Had he not a wife? Had he not children? Yes, for I too use the same language to you, as you do to me. He had a wife, but it was not because he had a wife that he was so remarkable. He had riches, but it was not because he had riches that he pleased God. He begat children, but it was not because he begat children that he was pronounced blessed. He had three hundred and eighteen servants born in his house, but it was not on this account that he was accounted wonderful. But would you know why it was? It was for his hospitality, for his contempt of riches, for his chastened conduct. For what, tell me, is the duty of a philosopher? Is it not to despise both riches and glory? Is it not to be above both envy and every other passion? Come now then, let us bring him forward and strip him, and show you what a philosopher he was. First of all, he esteemed his fatherland as nothing. God said, "Get thee out of thy country, and from thy kindred" (Gen. xii. 1.), and immediately he went forth. He was not bound to his house, (or surely he would never have gone forth,) nor to his love of familiar friends, nor to anything else whatever. But what? glory and money he despised above all others. For when he had put an end to war by turning the enemy to flight, and was requested to take the spoil, he rejected it. (Gen. xiv. 21–23.)

Again, the son of this great man was reverenced, not because of his riches, but for his hospitality: not because of his children, but for his obedience: not because of his wife, but for the barrenness inflicted on his wife. (Gen. xxv. 21.)

They looked upon the present life as nothing, they followed not after gain, they despised all things. Tell me, which sort of plants are the best? Are not those which have their strength from themselves and are injured neither by rains, nor by hailstorms, nor by gusts of wind, nor by any other vicissitude of the sort, but stand naked in defiance of them all, and needing neither wall nor fence to protect them? Such is the true philosopher, such is that wealth of which we spoke. He has nothing, and has all things: he has all things, and has nothing. For a fence is not within, but only without; a wall is not a thing of nature, but only built round from without. And what again, I ask, what sort of body is a strong one? Is it not that which is in health, and which is overcome neither by hunger nor repletion, nor by cold, nor by heat; or is it that which in view of all these things, needs both caterers, and weavers, and hunters, and physicians, to give it health? He is the rich man, the true philosopher, who needeth none of these things. For this cause it was that this blessed Apostle said, "Bring them up in the chastening and admonition of the Lord." Surround them not with outward defenses. For such is wealth, such is glory; for when these fall, and they do fall, the plant stands naked and defenseless, not only having derived no profit from them during the time past, but even injury. For those very shelters that prevented its being inured to the attacks of the winds, will now have prepared it for perishing all at once. And so wealth is injurious rather, because it renders us undisciplined for the vicissitudes of life. Let us therefore train up our children to be such, that they shall be able to bear up against every trial, and not be surprised at what may come upon them; "let us bring them up in the chastening and admonition of the Lord." And great will be the reward which will be thus laid up in store for us. For if men for making statues and painting portraits of kings enjoy so great honor, shall not we who adorn the image of the King of kings, (for man is the image of God,) receive ten thousand blessings, if we effect a true likeness? For the likeness is in this, in the virtue of the soul, when we train our children to be good, to be meek, to be forgiving, (because all these are attributes of God,) to be beneficent, to be humane; when we train them to regard the present world as nothing. Let this then be our task, to mold and to direct both ourselves and them according to what is right. Otherwise with what sort of boldness shall we stand before the judgment-seat of Christ? If a man who has unruly children is unworthy to be a Bishop (Tit. i. 6.), much more is he unworthy of the kingdom of Heaven. What sayest thou? If we have an unruly wife, or unruly children, shall we have to render account? Yes, we shall, if we do not with exactness bring in that which is due from ourselves; for our own individual virtue is not enough in order to salvation. If the man who laid aside the one talent gained nothing, but was punished even in such a manner, it is plain that one's own individual virtue is not enough in order to salvation, but there is need of that of another also. Let us therefore entertain great solicitude for our wives, and take great care of our children, and of our servants, and of ourselves. And in our government both of ourselves and of them, let us beseech God that He aid us in the work. If He shall see us interested in this work, and solicitous about it, He will aid us; but if He shall see us paying no regard to it, He will not give us His hand. For He does not vouchsafe us

His assistance when we sleep, but when we labor also ourselves. For a helper, (as the name implies,) is not a helper of one that is inactive, but of one who works also himself. But the good God is able of Himself to bring the work to perfection, that we may be all counted worthy to attain to the blessings promised us, through the grace and compassions of His only begotten Son, with Whom together with the Holy Ghost be unto the Father, glory, might, and honor, now and ever, and throughout all ages.

Amen.

---

1. Cf. Nicene and Post-Nicene Fathers: Series I, Volume XIII: Homilies on Galatians, Ephesians, Philippians, Colossians, Thessalonians, Timothy, Titus, and Philemon / On Ephesians / Homily XXI.

COLOSSIANS IV. 12, 13

(Homily XII[1])

Epaphras, who is one of you, a servant of Christ
Jesus, saluteth you, always striving for you in his
prayers, that ye may stand perfect and fully
assured in all the will of God. For I bear him
witness, that he hath much zeal for you, and for
them in Laodicea, and for them in Hierapolis.

In the commencement of this Epistle also, he
commended this man for his love; for even
to praise is a sign of love; thus in the beginning he said, "Who also declared unto us your
love in the Spirit." (Col. i. 8.) To pray for one is
also a sign of love, and causeth love again. He
commends him moreover in order to open a door

to his teachings, for reverendness in the teacher is the disciples' advantage; and so again is his saying, "one of you," in order that they might pride themselves upon the man, as producing such men. And he saith, "always striving for you in prayers." He said not simply "praying," but "striving," trembling and fearing. "For I bear him witness," he saith, "that he hath much zeal for you." A trustworthy witness. "That he hath," he saith, "much zeal for you," that is, that he loveth you exceedingly; and burneth with passionate affection for you. "And them in Laodicea, and them in Hierapolis." He commendeth him to those also. But whence were they to know this? They would assuredly have heard; however, they would also learn it when the Epistle was read. For he said, "Cause that it be read also in the church of the Laodiceans." "That ye may stand perfect," he saith. At once he both accuseth them, and without offensiveness gives them advice and counsel. For it is possible both to be perfect, and withal not to stand, as if one were to know all, and still be wavering; it is possible also not to be perfect, and yet to stand, as if one were to know a part, and stand [not] firmly. But this man prayeth for both: "That ye may stand perfect," he saith. See how again he has reminded them of what he said about the Angels, and about life. "And fully assured," he saith, "in all the will of God." It is not enough, simply to do His will. He that is "filled," suffereth not any other will to be within him, for if so, he is not wholly filled. "For I bear him witness," he saith, "that he hath much zeal." Both "zeal," and "great"; both are intensitive. As he saith himself, when writing to the Corinthians, "For I am jealous over you with a godly jealousy." (2 Cor. xi. 2.)

Ver. 14. "Luke, the beloved physician, saluteth you." This is the Evangelist. It is not to lower this man that he placeth him after, but to raise the other, viz. Epaphroditus. It is probable that there were others called by this name. "And Demas," he says. After saying, "Luke, the physician, saluteth you," he added, "the beloved." And no small praise is this, but even great exceedingly, to be beloved of Paul.

Ver. 15. "Salute the brethren that are in Laodicea, and Nymphas, and the Church that is in their house."

See how he cements, and knits them together with one another, not by salutation only, but also by interchanging his Epistles. Then again he pays a compliment by addressing him individually. And this he doth not without a reason, but in order to lead the others also to emulate his zeal. For it is not a small thing not to be numbered with the rest. Mark further how he shows the man to be great, seeing his house was a church.

Ver. 14. "And when this Epistle hath been read

among you, cause that it be read also in the church of the Laodiceans." I suppose there are some of the things therein written, which it was needful that those also should hear. And they would have the greater advantage of recognizing their own errors in the charges brought against others.

"And that ye also read the Epistle from Laodicea." Some say that this is not Paul's to them, but theirs to Paul, for he said not that to the Laodiceans, but that written "from Laodicea."

Ver. 17. "And say to Archippus, Take heed to the ministry which thou hast received in the Lord, that thou fulfill it." Wherefore doth he not write to him? Perhaps he needed it not, but only a bare reminding, so as to be more diligent.

Ver. 18. "The salutation of me, Paul, with mine own hand." This is a proof of their sincerity and affection; that they both looked at his handwriting, and that with emotion. "Remember my bonds." Wonderful! How great the consolation! For this is enough to cheer them on to all things, and make them bear themselves more nobly in their trials; but he made them not only the braver, but also the more nearly interested. "Grace be with you. Amen."

It is great praise, and greater than all the rest, his saying of Epaphras, "who is [one] of you, a servant of Christ." And he calleth him a minister for them, like as he termeth himself also a minister of the Church, as when he saith, "Whereof I Paul was made a minister." (Col. i. 23.) To the same dignity he advances this man; and above he calleth him a "fellow-servant" (Col. i. 7.), and here, "a servant." "Who is of you," he saith, as if speaking to a mother, and saying, "who is of thy womb." But this praise might have gendered envy; therefore he commendeth him not from these things only, but also from what had regard to themselves; and so he does away with envy, both in the former place, and here. "Always," he saith, "striving for you," not now only, whilst with us, to make a display; nor yet only whilst with you, to make a display before you. By saying, "striving," he hath showed his great earnestness. Then, that he might not seem to be flattering them, he added, "that he hath much zeal for you, and for them in Laodicea, and for them in Hierapolis." And the words, "that ye may stand perfect," are not words of flattery, but of a reverend teacher. Both "fully assured" he saith, "and perfect." The one he granted them, the other he said was lacking. And he said not, "that ye be not shaken," but, "that ye may stand." Their being saluted, however, by many, is refreshing to them, seeing that not only their friends from among themselves; but others also, remember them.

"And say to Archippus, Take heed to the ministry which thou hast received in the Lord." His chief aim is to subject them to him entirely. For they could no more have complaint against him for rebuking them, when they themselves had taken it all upon them; for it is not reasonable to talk to the disciples about the teacher. But to stop their mouths, he writes thus to them; "Say to Archippus," he saith, "Take heed." This word is everywhere used to alarm; as when he saith, "Take heed of dogs." (Philip. iii. 2.) "Take heed lest there shall be any one that maketh spoil of you." (Col. ii. 8.) "Take heed lest by any means this liberty of yours become a stumblingblock to the weak." (1 Cor. viii. 9.) And he always so expresses himself when he would terrify. "Take heed," he saith, "to the ministry which thou hast received in the Lord, that thou fulfill it." He doth not even allow him the power of choosing, as he saith himself, "For if I do this of mine own will, I have a reward: but if not of mine own will, I have a stewardship entrusted to me." (1 Cor. ix. 17.) "That thou fulfill it," continually using diligence. "Which thou hast received in the Lord, that thou fulfill it." Again, the word "in" means "through the Lord." He gave it thee, says he, not we. He subjects them also to him, when he shows that they had been committed to his hands by God.

"Remember my bonds. Grace be with you. Amen." He hath released their terror. For although their teacher be in bonds, yet "grace" releaseth him. This too is of grace, the granting him to be put in bonds. For hear Luke saying, The Apostles returned "from the presence of the council, rejoicing that they were counted worthy to suffer dishonor for the Name." (Acts v. 41.) For both to suffer shame, and to be put in bonds, is indeed to be "counted worthy." For, if he that hath one whom he loveth, deemeth it gain to suffer aught for his sake, much rather then is it so to suffer for the sake of Christ. Repine we not then at our tribulations for Christ's sake, but let us also remember Paul's bonds, and be this our incitement. For instance: dost thou exhort any to give to the poor for Christ's sake? Remind them of Paul's bonds, and bemoan thy misery and theirs, seeing that he indeed gave up even his body to bonds for His sake, but thou wilt not give a portion even of thy food. Art thou lifted up because of thy good deeds? Remember Paul's bonds, that thou hast suffered nought of that kind, and thou wilt be lifted up no more. Covetest thou any of the things that are thy neighbor's? Remember Paul's bonds, and thou wilt see how unreasonable it is, that whilst he was in perils, thou shouldest be in delights. Again, is thine heart set upon self-indulgence? Picture to thy mind Paul's prison-house; thou art his disciple, his fellow-soldier. How is it reasonable, that thy fellow-soldier should be in bonds, and thou in luxury? Art thou in affliction? Dost thou deem thyself forsaken? Hear Paul's bonds, and thou wilt see, that to be in affliction is no proof of being forsaken. Wouldest thou wear silken robes? Remember Paul's bonds; and these things will appear to thee more worthless than the filth-bespattered rags of her that sitteth apart. Wouldest thou array thee with golden trinkets? Picture to thy mind Paul's bonds, and these things will seem to thee no better than a withered bulrush. Wouldest thou tire thine hair, and be beautiful to see? Think of Paul's squalidness within that prison-house, and thou wilt burn for that beauty, and deem this the extreme of ugliness, and wilt groan bitterly through longing for those bonds. Wouldest thou daub thee with pastes and pigments, and such like things? Think of his tears: a three-years space, night and day, he ceased not to weep. (Acts xx. 31.) With this adorning deck thy cheek; these tears do make it bright. I say not, that thou weep for others, (I wish indeed it could be even so, but this is too high for thee,) but for thine own sins I advise thee to do this. Hast thou ordered thy slave to be put in bonds, and wast thou angry, and exasperated? Remember Paul's bonds, and thou wilt straightway stay thine anger; remember that we are of the bound, not the binders, of the bruised in heart, not the bruisers. Hast thou lost self-control, and shouted loud in laughter?

Think of his lamentations, and thou wilt groan; such tears will show thee brighter far. Seest thou any persons rioting and dancing? Remember his tears. What fountain has gushed forth so great streams as those eyes did tears? "Remember my tears" (Acts xx. 31.), he saith, as here "bonds." And with reason he spoke thus to them, when he sent for them from Ephesus to Miletus. For he was then speaking to teachers. He demands of those therefore, that they should sympathize also, but of these that they should only encounter dangers.

What fountain wilt thou compare to these tears? That in Paradise, which watereth the whole earth? But thou wilt have mentioned nothing like it. For this fount of tears watered souls, not earth. If one were to show us Paul bathed in tears, and groaning, would not this be better far to see, than countless choirs gayly crowned? I am not now speaking of you; but, if one, having pulled away from the theater and the stage some wanton fellow, burning and drunken with carnal love, were to show him a young virgin in the very flower of her age, surpassing her fellows, both in other respects, and in her face more than the rest of her person, having an eye, tender and soft, that gently resteth, and gently rolleth, moist, mild, calmly smiling, and arrayed in much modesty and much grace, fringed with dark lashes both under and over, having an eyeball, so to speak, alive, a forehead radiant; underneath, again, a cheek shaded to exact redness, lying smooth as marble, and even; and then any one should show me Paul weeping; leaving that maiden, I would have eagerly sprung away to the sight of him; for from his eyes there beamed spiritual beauty. For that other transporteth the souls of youths, it scorcheth and inflameth them; but this, on the contrary, subdueth them. This maketh the eyes of the soul more beauteous, it curbeth the belly: it filleth with the love of wisdom, with much sympathy: and it is able to soften even a soul of adamant. With these tears the Church is watered, with these souls are planted; yea, though there be fire sensible and substantial, yet can these tears quench it; these tears quench the fiery darts of the wicked one.

Remember we then these tears of his, and we shall laugh to scorn all present things. These tears did Christ pronounce blessed, saying, "Blessed are they that mourn, and blessed are they that weep, for they shall laugh." (Matt. v. 4; Luke vi. 21.) Such tears did Isaiah too, and Jeremiah weep; and the former said, "Leave me alone, I will weep bitterly" (Isa. xxii. 4, Sept.): and the latter, "Who will give my head water, and mine eyes fountains of tears?" (Jer. ix. 1.); as though the natural fount were not enough.

Nothing is sweeter than these tears; sweeter are they than any laughter. They that mourn, know how great consolation it possesseth. Let us not think this a thing to be deprecated, but one to be even exceedingly prayed for; not that others may sin, but that, when they sin, we may be heart-broken for them. Remember we these tears, these bonds. Surely too upon those bonds tears descended; but the death of the perishing, of those that had bound him in them, suffered him not to taste the pleasure of the bonds. For in their behalf he grieved, being a disciple of Him that bewept the priests of the Jews; not because they were going to crucify Him, but because they were themselves perishing. And He doeth not this Himself alone, but He thus exhorteth others also, saying, "Daughters of Jerusalem, weep not for Me." (Luke xxiii. 28.) These eyes saw Paradise, saw the third heaven: but I count not them so blessed because of this sight, as because of those tears, through which they saw Christ. Blessed, indeed, was that sight; for he himself even glories in it, saying, "Have I not seen Jesus Christ our Lord?" (1 Cor. ix. 1.); but more blessed so to weep.

In that sight many have been partakers, and those who have not so been, Christ the rather calls blessed, saying, "Blessed are they that have not seen, and yet have believed" (John xx. 29.); but unto this not many have attained. For if to stay here for Christ's sake were more needful than to depart to Him (Philip. i. 23, 24.), for the sake of the salvation of others; surely then to groan for others' sakes, is more needful even than to see Him. For if for His sake to be in hell, is rather to be desired, than to be with Him; and to be separated from Him for His sake more to be desired than to be with Him, (for this is what he said, "For I could wish that I myself were anathema from Christ" (Rom. ix. 3.), much more is weeping for His sake. "I ceased not," he saith, "to admonish everyone with tears." (Acts xx. 31.) Wherefore? Not fearing the dangers; no; but as if one sitting by a sick man's side, and not knowing what would be the end, should weep for affection, fearing lest he should lose his life; so too did he; when he saw any one diseased, and could not prevail by rebuke, he thenceforward wept. So did Christ also, that happily they might reverence His tears: thus, one sinned, He rebuked him; the rebuked spat upon Him, and sprang aloof; He wept, that haply He might win him even so.

Remember we these tears: thus let us bring up our daughters, thus our sons; weeping when we see them in evil. As many women as wish to be loved, let them remember Paul's tears, and groan: as many of you as are counted blest, as many as are in bridal chambers, as many as are in pleasure, remember these; as many as are in mourning, exchange tears for tears. He mourned not for the dead; but for those that were perishing whilst alive. Shall I tell of other tears? Timothy also wept; for he was this man's disciple; wherefore also when writing to him he said, "Remembering thy tears, that I may be filled with joy." (2 Tim. i. 4.) Many weep even from pleasure. So it is also a matter of pleasure, and that of the utmost intensity. So the tears are not painful: yea, the tears that flow from such sorrow are even better far than those due to worldly pleasure. Hear the Prophet saying, "The Lord hath heard the voice of my weeping, he hath heard the voice of my supplication." (Ps. vi. 8.) For where is the tear not useful? in prayers? in exhortations? We get them an ill name, by using them not to what they are given us for. When we entreat a sinning brother, we ought to weep, grieving and groaning; when we exhort any one, and he giveth us no heed, but goeth on perishing, we ought to weep. These are the tears of heavenly wisdom. When however one is in poverty, or bodily disease, or dead, not so; for these are not things worthy of tears.

As then we gain an ill name for laughter also, when we use it out of season; so too do we for tears, by having recourse to them unseasonably. For the virtue of each thing then discovers itself when it is brought to its own fitting work, but when to one that is alien, it doth no longer so. For instance, wine is given for cheerfulness, not drunkenness, bread for nourishment, sexual intercourse for the procreation of children. As then these things have gained an ill name, so also have tears. Be there a law laid down, that they be used in prayers and exhortations only, and see how desirable a thing they will become. Nothing doth so wipe out sins, as tears. Tears show even this bodily countenance beautiful; for they win the spectator to pity, they make it respected in our eyes. Nothing is sweeter than tearful eyes. For this is the noblest member we have, and the most beautiful, and the soul's own. And therefore we are so bowed therewith, as though we saw the soul itself lamenting.

I have not spoken these things without a reason; but in order that ye may cease your attendance at weddings, at dancings, at Satanical performances. For see what the devil hath invented. Since nature itself hath withheld women from the stage, and the disgraceful things enacted there, he hath introduced into the women's apartment the furniture of the theater, I mean, wanton men and harlots. This pestilence the custom of marriages hath introduced, or rather, not of marriages, far be it, but of our own silliness. What is it thou doest, O man? Dost thou not know what thou art at? Thou marriest a wife for chastity, and procreation of children; what then mean these harlots? That there may be, one answereth, greater gladness. And yet is not this rather madness?

Thou insultest thy bride, thou insultest the women that are invited. For if they are delighted with such proceedings, the thing is an insult. If to see harlots acting indecorously conferreth any honor, wherefore dost thou not drag thy bride also thither, that she too may see? It is quite indecent and disgraceful to introduce into one's house lewd fellows and dancers, and all that Satanic pomp.

"Remember," he saith, "my bonds." Marriage is a bond, a bond ordained of God, a harlot is a severing and a dissolving. It is permitted you to embellish marriage with other things, such as full tables, and apparel. I do not cut off these things, lest I should seem to be clownish to an extreme; and yet Rebecca was content with her veil only (Gen. xxiv. 65.); still I do not cut them off. It is permitted you to embellish and set off marriage with apparel, with the presence of reverend men and reverend women. Why introducest thou those mockeries? why those monsters? Tell us what it is thou hearest from them? What? dost thou blush to tell? Dost thou blush, and yet force them to do it? If it is honorable, wherefore dost thou not do it thyself as well? but if disgraceful, wherefore dost thou compel another? Everything should be full of chasteness, of gravity, of orderliness; but I see the reverse, people frisking like camels and mules. For the virgin, her chamber is the only befitting place. "But," saith one, "she is poor." Because she is poor, she ought to be modest also; let her have her character in the place of a fortune. Has she no dowry to give with herself? Then why dost thou make her otherwise contemptible through her life and manners? I praise the custom, that virgins attend to do honor to their fellow; matrons attend to do honor to her who is made one of their order. Rightly hath this been ordered. For these are two companies, one of virgins, the other of the married; the one are giving her up, the other receiving her. The bride is between them, neither virgin, nor wife, for she is coming forth from those, and entering into the fellowship of these. But those harlots, what mean they? They ought to hide their faces when marriage is celebrated; they ought to be dug into the earth, (for harlotry is the corruption of marriage,) but we introduce them at our marriages. And, when ye are engaged in any work, ye count it ill-omened to speak even a syllable of what is adverse to it; for instance, when thou sowest, when thou drawest off the wine from thy vats, thou wouldest not, even if asked, utter a syllable about vinegar; but here, where the object is chasteness, introduce ye the vinegar? for such is an harlot. When ye are preparing sweet ointment, ye suffer nought ill-scented to be near. Marriage is a sweet ointment. Why then introducest thou the foul stench of the dunghill into the preparation of thy ointment? What sayest thou? Shall the virgin dance, and yet feel no shame before her fellow? For she ought to have more gravity than the other; she hath at least come forth from the [nurse's] arm, and not from the palæstra. For the virgin ought not to appear publicly at all at a marriage.

Seest thou not how in kings' houses, the honored are within, about the king, the unhonored without? Do thou too be within about the bride. But remain in the house in chasteness, expose not thy virginity. Either company is standing by, the one to show of what sort she is whom they are giving up, the other in order that they may guard her. Why disgracest thou the virgin estate? For if thou art such as this, the same will the bridegroom suspect her to be. If thou wishest to have men in love with thee, this is the part of saleswomen, green-grocers, and handicrafts-people. Is not this a shame? To act unseemly is a shame even though it be a king's daughter. For doth her poverty stand in the way? or her course of life? Even if a virgin be a slave, let her abide in modesty. "For in Christ Jesus there can be neither bond nor free." (Gal. iii. 28.)

What? is marriage a theater? It is a mystery and a type of a mighty thing; and even if thou reverence not it, reverence that whose type it is. "This mystery," saith he, "is great, but I speak in regard of Christ and of the Church." (Eph. v. 32.) It is a type of the Church, and of Christ, and dost thou introduce harlots at it? If then, saith one, neither virgins dance, nor the married, who is to dance? No one, for what need is there of dancing? In the Grecian mysteries there are dancings, but in ours, silence and decency, modesty, and bashfulness. A great mystery is being celebrated: forth with the harlots! forth with the profane! How is it a mystery? They come together, and the two make one. Wherefore is it that at his entrance indeed, there was no dancing, no cymbals, but great silence, great stillness; but when they come together, making not a lifeless image, nor yet the image of anything upon earth, but of God Himself, and after his likeness, thou introducest so great an uproar, and disturbest those that are there, and puttest the soul to shame, and confoundest it? They come, about to be made one body. See again a mystery of love! If the two become not one, so long as they continue two, they make not many, but when they are come into oneness, they then make many. What do we learn from this? That great is the power of union. The wise counsel of God at the beginning divided the one into two; and being desirous of showing that even after division it remaineth still one, He suffered not that the one should be of itself enough for procreation. For he is not one who is not yet [united,] but the half of one; and it is evident from this, that he begetteth no offspring, as was the case also beforetime. Seest thou the mystery of marriage? He made of one, one; and again, having made these two, one, He so maketh one, so that now also man is produced of one. For man and wife are not two men, but one Man. And this may be confirmed from many sources; for instance, from James, from Mary the Mother of Christ, from the words, "He made them male and female." (Gen. i. 27.) If he be the head, and she the body, how are they two? Therefore the one holdeth the rank of a disciple, the other of a teacher, the one of a ruler, the other of a subject. Moreover, from the very fashioning of her body, one may see that they are one, for she was made from his side, and they are, as it were, two halves.

For this cause He also calleth her a help, to show that they are one (Gen. ii. 18.); for this cause He honoreth their cohabitation beyond both father and mother, to show that they are one. (Gen. ii. 24.) And in like manner a father rejoiceth both when son and daughter marry, as though the body were hastening to join a member of its own; and though so great a charge and expenditure of money is incurred still he cannot bear with indifference to see her unmarried. For as though her own flesh itself were severed from her, each one separately is imperfect for the procreation of children, each one is imperfect as regards the constitution of this present life. Wherefore also the Prophet saith, "the residue of thy spirit." (Mal. ii. 15, Sept.) And how become they one flesh? As if thou shouldest take away the purest part of gold, and mingle it with other gold; so in truth here also the woman as it were receiving the richest part fused by pleasure, nourisheth it and cherisheth it, and withal contributing her own share, restoreth it back a Man. And the child is a sort of bridge, so that the three become one flesh, the child connecting, on either side, each to other. For like as two cities, which a river divides throughout, become one, if a bridge connect them on both sides, so is it in this case; and yet more, when the very bridge in this case is formed of the substance of each. As the body and the head are one body; for they are divided by the neck; but not divided more than connected, for it, lying between them brings together each with the other. And it is the same as if a chorus that had been severed should, by taking one part of itself from this quarter, and the other again from the right, make one; or as these when come into close rank, and extending hands, become one; for the hands extended admit not of their being two. Therefore to wit He said with accuracy of expression, not "they shall be one flesh" but joined together "into one flesh" (Gen. ii. 2, Sept.), namely, that of the child. What then? when there is no child, will they not be two? Nay, for their coming together hath this effect, it diffuses and commingles the bodies of both. And as one who hath cast ointment into oil, hath made the whole one; so in truth is it also here.

I know that many are ashamed at what is said, and the cause of this is what I spoke of, your own lasciviousness, and unchasteness. The fact of marriages being thus performed, thus depraved, hath gained the thing an ill name: for "marriage is honorable, and the bed undefiled." (Heb. xiii. 4.) Why art thou ashamed of the honorable, why blushest thou at the undefiled? This is for heretics, this is for such as introduce harlots thither. For this cause I am desirous of having it thoroughly purified, so as to bring it back again to its proper nobleness, so as to stop the mouths of the heretics. The gift of God is insulted, the root of our generation; for about that root there is much dung and filth. This then let us cleanse away by our discourse. Endure then a little while, for he that holdeth filth must endure the stench. I wish to show you that ye ought not to be ashamed at these things, but at those which ye do; but thou, passing by all shame at those, art ashamed at these; surely then thou condemnest God who hath thus decreed.

Shall I tell how marriage is also a mystery of the Church? As Christ came into the Church, and she was made of him, and he united with her in a spiritual intercourse, "for," saith one, "I have espoused you to one husband, a pure virgin." (2 Cor. xi. 2.) And that we are of Him, he saith, of His members, "and of His flesh." Thinking then on all these things, let us not cast shame upon so great a mystery. Marriage is a type of the presence of Christ, and art thou drunken at it? Tell me; if thou sawest an image of the king, wouldest thou dishonor it? By no means.

Now the practices at marriages seem to be a matter of indifference, but they are the causes of great mischiefs. All is full of lawlessness. "Filthiness, and foolish talking, and jesting, let it not proceed," saith he, "out of your mouth." (Eph. v. 4; iv. 29.) Now all these things are filthiness, foolish talking, and jesting; and not these simply, but with aggravation, for the thing has become an art, and there are great praises for those that pursue it. Sins have become an art! We pursue them not in any chance way, but with earnestness, with science, and thenceforth the devil takes the command of his own array. For where drunkenness is, there is unchasteness: where filthy talking, there the devil is at hand bringing in his own contributions; with such an entertainment, tell me, dost thou celebrate the mystery of Christ? and invitest thou the devil?

I dare say you consider me offensive. For this too is a property of extreme pervertedness, that even one that rebuketh you incurs your ridicule as one that is austere. Hear ye not Paul, saying, "Whatsoever ye do, whether ye eat or drink or whatsoever ye do, do all to the glory of God"? (1 Cor. x. 31.) But ye do all to ill report and dishonor. Hear ye not the Prophet, saying, "Serve the Lord with fear, and rejoice unto Him with trembling?" (Ps. ii. 11.) But ye are wholly without restraint. Is it not possible both to enjoy pleasure, and to do so with safety? Art thou desirous of hearing beautiful songs? Best of all indeed, thou oughtest not; nevertheless, I condescend if thou wilt have it so: do not hear those Satanic ones, but the spiritual. Art thou desirous of seeing choirs of dancers? Behold the choir of Angels. And how is it possible, saith one, to see them? If thou drive away all these things, even Christ will come to such a marriage, and Christ being present, the choir of Angels is present also. If thou wilt, He will even now work miracles as He did then; He will make even now the water, wine (John ii.); and what is much more wonderful, He will convert this unstable and dissolving pleasure, this cold desire, and change it into the spiritual. This is to make of water, wine. Where pipers are, by no means there is Christ; but even if He should have entered, He first casts these forth, and then He works His wonders. What can be more disagreeable than this Satanic pomp? where everything is inarticulate, everything without significancy; and if there be anything articulate, again all is shameful, all is noisome.

Nothing is more pleasurable than virtue, nothing sweeter than orderliness, nothing more amiable than gravity. Let any celebrate such a marriage as I speak of; and he shall find the pleasure; but what sort of marriages these are, take heed. First seek a husband for the virgin, who will be truly a husband, and a protector; as though thou wert intending to place a head upon a body; as though about to give not a slave, but a daughter into his hands. Seek not money, nor splendor of family, nor greatness of country; all these things are superfluous; but piety of soul, gentleness, the true understanding, the fear of God, if thou wishest thy darling to live with pleasure. For if thou seek a wealthier husband, not only wilt thou not benefit her, but thou wilt even harm her, by making her a slave instead of free. For the pleasure she will reap from her golden trinkets will not be so great as will be the annoyance that comes of her slavery. I pray thee, seek not these things, but most of all, one of equal condition; if however this cannot be, rather one poorer than in better circumstances; if at least thou be desirous not of selling thy daughter to a master, but of giving her to a husband. When thou hast thoroughly investigated the virtue of the man, and art about to give her to him, beseech Christ to be present: for He will not be ashamed to be so; it is the mystery of His presence. Yea rather beseech Him even in the first instance, to grant her such a suitor. Be not worse than the servant of Abraham, who, when sent on a pilgrimage so important, saw whither he ought to have recourse; wherefore also he obtained everything. When thou art taking anxious pains, and seeking a husband for her, pray; say unto God, "whomsoever Thou wilt do Thou provide:" into His hands commit the matter; and He, honored in this way by thee, will requite thee with honor.

Two things indeed it is necessary to do; to commit the thing into His hands, and to seek such an orderly person as He Himself approves.

When then thou makest a marriage, go not round from house to house borrowing mirrors and dresses; for the matter is not one of display, nor dost thou lead thy daughter to a pageant; but decking out thine house with what is in it, invite thy neighbors, and friends, and kindred. As many as thou knowest to be of a good character, those invite, and bid them be content with what there is. Let no one from the orchestra be present, for such expense is superfluous, and unbecoming. Before all the rest, invite Christ. Knowest thou whereby thou wilt invite Him? Whosoever, saith He, "hath done it to one of these least, hath done it to Me."

(Matt. xxv. 40.) And think it not an annoying thing to invite the poor for Christ's sake; to invite harlots is an annoyance. For to invite the poor is a means of wealth, the other of ruin. Adorn the bride not with these ornaments that are made of gold, but with gentleness and modesty, and the customary robes; in place of all golden ornament and braiding, arraying her in blushes, and shamefacedness, and the not desiring such things. Let there be no uproar, no confusion; let the bridegroom be called, let him receive the virgin. The dinners and suppers, let them not be full of drunkenness, but of abundance and pleasure. See how many good things will result, whenever we see such marriages as those; but from the marriages that are now celebrated, (if at least one ought to call them marriages and not pageants,) how many are the evils! The banquet hall is no sooner broken up, than straightway comes care and fear, lest aught that is borrowed should have been lost, and there succeeds to the pleasure melancholy intolerable. But this distress belongs to the mother-in-law,—nay, rather not even is the bride herself free; all that follows at least belongs to the bride herself. For to see all broken up, is a ground for sadness, to see the house desolate.

There is Christ, here is Satan; there is cheerfulness, here anxious care; there pleasure, here pain; there expense, here nothing of the kind; there indecency, here modesty; there envy, here no envy; there drunkenness, here soberness, here health, here temperance. Bearing in mind all these things, let us stay the evil at this point, that we may please God, and be counted worthy to obtain the good things promised to them that love Him, through the grace and love toward man of our Lord Jesus Christ, with whom, to the Father, together with the Holy Ghost, be glory, power, honor, now and for ever, and world without end. Amen.

---

1. Cf. Nicene and Post-Nicene Fathers: Series I / Volume XIII : On Philippians, Colossians, and Thessalonians / On Colossians / Homily XII.

MATT. V. 27, 28.

(Homily XVII[1])

Ye have heard that it was said to them of old time, Thou shalt not commit adultery; but I say unto you, that every one who looketh upon a woman to lust after her, hath committed adultery with her already in his heart.

Having now finished the former commandment, and having extended it unto the height of self-denial, He, advancing in course and order, proceeds accordingly unto the second, herein too obeying the law.

"And yet," it may be said, "this is not the second, but the third; for neither is the first, "Thou shalt not kill," but "The Lord thy God is one Lord."

Wherefore it is worth inquiring too, why He did not begin with that. Why was it then? Because, had He begun from thence, He must have enlarged it also, and have brought in Himself together with His Father.

But it was not as yet time to teach any such thing about Himself.

And besides, He was for a while practising His moral doctrine only, being minded from this first, and from His miracles, to convince the hearers that He was the Son of God. Now, if He had said at once, before He had spoken or done anything, "Ye have heard that it was said to them of old time, "I am the Lord thy God, and there is none other but me," but I say unto you, Worship me even as Him; this would have made all regard Him as a madman. For if, even after His teaching, and His so great miracles, while not even yet was He saying this openly, they called Him possessed with a devil; had He before all these attempted to say any such thing, what would they not have said? what would they not have thought?

But by keeping back at the proper season His teaching on these subjects, He was causing that the doctrine should be acceptable to the many. Wherefore now He passed it by quickly, but when He had everywhere established it by His miracles, and by His most excellent teaching, He afterwards unveiled it in words also.

For the present, however, by the manifestation of His miracles, and by the very manner of His teaching, He unfolds it on occasion, gradually and quietly. For His enacting such laws, and such corrections of laws, with authority, would lead on the attentive and understanding hearer, by little and little, unto the word of His doctrine. For it is said, "they were astonished at Him, because He taught not as their Scribes."

2. For beginning from those passions, which most belong to our whole race, anger, I mean, and desire (for it is these chiefly that bear absolute sway within us, and are more natural than the rest); He with great authority, even such as became a legislator, both corrected them, and reduced them to order with all strictness. For He said not that the adulterer merely is punished; but what He had done with respect to the murderer, this He doth here also, punishing even the unchaste look: to teach thee wherein lies what He had more than the scribes. Accordingly, He saith, "He that looketh upon a woman to lust after her hath already committed adultery with her:" that is, he who makes it his business to be curious about bright forms, and to hunt for elegant features, and to feast his soul with the sight, and to fasten his eyes on fair countenances. For He came

to set free from all evil deeds not the body only, but the soul too before the body. Thus, because in the heart we receive the grace of the Spirit, He cleanses it out first.

"And how," one may say, "is it possible to be freed from desire?" I answer, first, if we were willing, even this might be deadened, and remain inactive.

In the next place, He doth not here take away desire absolutely, but that desire which springs up in men from sight. For he that is curious to behold fair countenances, is himself chiefly the enkindler of the furnace of that passion, and makes his own soul a captive, and soon proceeds also to the act.

Thus we see why He said not, "whosoever shall lust to commit adultery," but, "whosoever shall look to lust." And in the case of anger He laid down a certain distinction, saying, "without a cause," and "for nought;" but here not so; rather once for all He took away the desire. Yet surely both are naturally implanted, and both are set in us for our profit; both anger, and desire: the one that we may chastise the evil, and correct those who walk disorderly; the other that we may have children, and that our race may be recruited by such successions.

Why then did He not make a distinction here also? Nay, very great is the distinction which, if thou attend, thou wilt see here also included. For

He said not simply, "whosoever shall desire," since it is possible for one to desire even when sitting in the mountains; but, "Whosoever shall look to lust;" that is to say, he who gathers in lust unto himself; he who, when nothing compels him, brings in the wild beast upon his thoughts when they are calm. For this comes no longer of nature, but of self-indulgence. This even the ancient Scripture corrects from the first, saying, "Contemplate not beauty which is another's." And then, lest any one should say, "what then, if I contemplate, and be not taken captive," He punishes the look, lest confiding in this security thou shouldest some time fall into sin. "What then," one may say, "if I should look, and desire indeed, but do no evil?" Even so thou art set among the adulterers. For the Lawgiver hath pronounced it, and thou must not ask any more questions. For thus looking once, twice, or thrice, thou wilt perhaps have power to refrain; but if thou art continually doing this, and kindling the furnace, thou wilt assuredly be taken; for thy station is not beyond that nature which is common to men. As we then, if we see a child holding a knife, though we do not see him hurt, beat him, and forbid his ever holding it; so God likewise takes away the unchaste look even before the act, lest at any time thou shouldest fall in act also. For he who hath once kindled the flame, even when the woman whom he hath beheld is absent, is forming by himself continually images of shameful things, and from them often goes on even to the deed. For this cause Christ takes away even that embrace which is in the heart only.

What now can they say, who have those virgin inmates? Why, by the tenor of this law they must be guilty of ten thousand adulteries, daily beholding them with desire. For this cause the blessed Job also laid down this law from the beginning, blocking out from himself on all sides this kind of gazing.

For in truth greater is the struggle on beholding, and not possessing the object of fondness: nor is the pleasure so great which we reap from the sight, as the mischief we undergo from increasing this desire; thus making our opponent strong, and giving more scope to the devil, and no longer able to repulse him, now that we have brought him into our inmost parts, and have thrown our mind open unto him. Therefore He saith, "commit no adultery with thine eyes, and thou wilt commit none with thy mind."

For one may indeed behold in another way, such as are the looks of the chaste; wherefore he did not altogether prohibit our seeing, but that seeing which is accompanied with desire. And if He had not meant this, He would have said simply, "He who looketh on a woman." But now He said not thus, but, "He who looketh to lust," "he who looketh to please his sight."

For not at all to this end did God make thee eyes, that thou shouldest thereby introduce adultery, but that, beholding His creatures, thou shouldest admire the Artificer.

Just then as one may feel wrath at random, so may one cast looks at random; that is, when thou doest it for lust. Rather, if thou desirest to look and find pleasure, look at thine own wife, and love her continually; no law forbids that. But if thou art to be curious about the beauties that belong to another, thou art injuring both thy wife by letting thine eyes wander elsewhere, and her on whom thou hast looked, by touching her unlawfully. Since, although thou hast not touched her with the hand, yet hast thou caressed her with thine eyes; for which cause this also is accounted adultery, and before that great penalty draws after it no slight one of its own. For then all within him is filled with disquiet and turmoil, and great is the tempest, and most grievous the pain, and no captive nor person in chains can be worse off than a man in this state of mind. And oftentimes she who hath shot the dart is flown away, while the wound even so remains. Or rather, it is not she who hath shot the dart, but thou gavest thyself the fatal wound, by thine unchaste look. And this I say to free modest women from the charge: since assuredly, should one deck herself out, and invite towards herself the eyes of such as fall in her way; even though she smite not him that meets with her, she incurs the utmost penalty: for she mixed the poison, she prepared the hemlock, even though she did not offer the cup. Or rather, she did also offer the cup, though no one were found to drink it.

3. "Why then doth He not discourse with them also?" it may be said. Because the laws which He appoints are in every case common, although He seem to address Himself unto men only. For in discoursing with the head, He makes His admonition common to the whole body also. For woman and man He knows as one living creature, and nowhere distinguishes their kind.

But if thou desirest to hear also His rebuke for them in particular, listen to Isaiah, in many words inveighing against them, and deriding their habit, their aspect, their gait, their trailing garments, their tripping feet, their drooping necks. Hear with him the blessed Paul also, setting many laws for them; and both *about garments, and* ornaments of gold, *and plaiting of hair, and luxurious living, and all other such things, vehemently rebuking this sex. And* Christ too, by what follows next, obscurely intimated this very same; for when He saith, "pluck out and cut off the eye that offendeth thee," He speaks as indicating His anger against them.

3. Wherefore also He subjoins, "If thy right eye offend thee, pluck it out, and cast it from thee."

Thus, lest thou shouldest say, "But what if she be akin to me? what if in any other way she belong to me?" therefore He hath given these injunctions; not discoursing about our limbs;—far from it,—for nowhere doth He say that our flesh is to be blamed for things, but everywhere it is the evil mind that is accused. For it is not the eye that sees, but the mind and the thought. Often, for instance, we being wholly turned elsewhere, our eye sees not those who are present. So that the matter does not entirely depend upon its working. Again, had He been speaking of members of the body, He would not have said it of one eye, nor of the right eye only, but of both. For he who is offended by his right eye, most evidently will incur the same evil by his left also. Why then did He mention the right eye, and add the hand? To show thee that not of limbs is He speaking, but of them who are near unto us. Thus, "If," saith He, "thou so lovest any one, as though he were in stead of a right eye; if thou thinkest him so profitable to thee as to esteem him in the place of a hand, and he hurts thy soul; even these do thou cut off." And see the emphasis; for He saith not, "Withdraw from him," but to show the fullness of the separation, "pluck it out," saith He, "and cast it from thee."

Then, forasmuch as His injunction was sharp, He shows also the gain on either hand, both from the benefits and from the evils, continuing in the metaphor.

"For it is profitable for thee," saith He, "that one of thy members should perish, and not that thy whole body should be cast into hell."

For while he neither saves himself, nor fails to destroy thee too, what kindness is it for both to sink, whereas if they were separated, one at least might have been preserved?

But why did Paul then, it may be said, choose to become accursed? Not on condition of gaining nothing, but with a view to the salvation of others. But in this case the mischief pertains to both. And therefore He said not, "pluck out" only, but also "cast from thee:" to receive him again no more, if he continue as he is. For so shalt thou both deliver him from a heavier charge, and free thyself from ruin.

But that thou mayest see yet more clearly the profit of this law; let us, if you please, try what hath been said, in the case of the body itself, by way of supposition. I mean, if choice were given, and thou must either, keeping thine eye, be cast into a pit and perish, or plucking it out, preserve the rest of thy body; wouldest thou not of course accept the latter? It is plain to everyone. For this were not to act as one hating the eye, but as one loving the rest of the body. This same reckoning do thou make with regard to men also and women: that if he who harms thee by his friendship should continue incurable, his being thus cut off will both free thee from all mischief, and he also will himself be delivered from the heavier charges, not having to answer for thy destruction along with his own evil deeds.

Seest thou how full the law is of gentleness and tender care, and that which seems to men in general to be severity, how much love towards man it discloses?

Let them hearken to these things, who hasten to the theatres, and make themselves adulterers every day. For if the law commands to cut off him, whose connexion with us tends to our hurt; what plea can they have, who, by their haunting those places, attract towards them daily those even that have not yet become known to them, and procure to themselves occasions of ruin without number?

For henceforth, He not only forbids us to look unchastely, but having signified the mischief thence ensuing, He even straitens the law as He goes on, commanding to cut off, and dissever, and cast somewhere far away. And all this He ordains, who hath uttered words beyond number about love, that in either way thou mightest learn His providence, and how from every source He seeks thy profit.

4. "Now it hath been said, Whosoever shall put away his wife, let him give her a writing of divorcement. But I say unto you, Whosoever shall put away his wife, saving for the cause of fornication, causeth her to commit adultery; and whosoever marrieth her that is put away, committeth adultery."

He goes not on to what lies before Him, until He have well cleared out the former topics. For, lo, He shows us yet another kind of adultery. And what is this? There was an ancient law made, that he who hated his wife, for whatever kind of cause, should not be forbidden to cast her out, and to bring home another instead of her. The law however did not command him simply to do this, but after giving the woman a writing of divorcement, that it might not be in her power to return to him again; that so at least the figure of the marriage might remain.

For if He had not enjoined this, but it were lawful first to cast her out, and take another, then afterwards to take back the former, the confusion was sure to be great, all men continually taking each others' wives; and the matter thenceforth would have been direct adultery. With a view to this, He devised, as no small mitigation, the writing of divorcement.

But these things were done by reason of another, a far greater wickedness; I mean, had He made it necessary to keep in the house her even that was hated, the husband, hating, would have killed her. For such was the race of the Jews. For they who did not spare children, who slew prophets, and "shed blood as water," much more would they have showed no mercy to women. For this cause He allowed the less, to remove the greater evil. For that this was not a primary law, hear Him saying, "Moses wrote these things according to the hardness of your hearts," that ye might not slay them in the house, but rather put them out. But forasmuch as He had taken away all wrath, having forbidden not murder only, but even the mere feeling of anger, He with ease introduces this law likewise. With this view also He is ever bringing to mind the former words, to signify that His sayings are not contrary to them, but in agreement: that He is enforcing, not overthrowing them; perfecting, not doing them away.

And observe Him everywhere addressing His discourse to the man. Thus, "He that putteth away his wife," saith He, "causeth her to commit adultery, and he that marrieth a woman put away, committeth adultery." That is, the former, though he take not another wife, by that act alone hath made himself liable to blame, having made the first an adulteress; the latter again is become an adulterer by taking her who is another's. For tell me not this, "the other hath cast her out;" nay, for when cast out she continues to be the wife of him that expelled her. Then lest He should render the wife more self-willed, by throwing it all upon him who cast her out, He hath shut against her also the doors of him who was afterwards receiving her; in that He saith, "He who marrieth her that is put away committeth adultery;" and so makes the woman chaste even though unwilling, and blocks up altogether her access to all, and suffers her not to give an occasion for jealousy. For she who hath been made aware that she positively must either keep the husband, who was originally allotted to her, or being cast out of that house, not have any other refuge;—she even against her will was compelled to make the best of her consort.

And if He discourse not at all unto her concerning these things, marvel not; for the woman is rather a weak creature. For this cause letting her go, in his threatening against the men He fully corrects her remissness. Just as if any one who had a prodigal child, leaving him, should rebuke those who make him such, and forbid them to have intercourse, or to approach him. And if that be galling, call to mind, I pray thee, His former sayings, on what terms He had blessed His hearers; and thou wilt see that it is very possible and easy. For he that is meek, and a peacemaker, and poor in spirit, and merciful, how shall he cast out his wife? He that is used to reconcile others, how shall he be at variance with her that is his own?

And not thus only, but in another way also He hath lightened the enactment: forasmuch as even for him He leaves one manner of dismissal, when He saith, "Except for the cause of fornication;" since the matter had else come round again to the same issue. For if He had commanded to keep her in the house, though defiling herself with many, He would have made the matter end again in adultery.

Seest thou how these sayings agree with what had gone before? For he who looks not with unchaste eyes upon another woman, will not commit whoredom; and not committing whoredom, he will give no occasion to the husband to cast out his wife.

Therefore, you see, after this He presses the point without reserve, and builds up this fear as a bulwark, urging on the husband the great danger, if he do cast her out, in that he makes himself accountable for her adultery. Thus, lest thou being told, "pluck out the eye," shouldest suppose this to be said even of a wife: He added in good time this corrective, in one way only giving leave to cast her out, but no otherwise.

5. "Again, ye have heard that it was said to them of old time, Thou shalt not forswear thyself,

but shalt perform unto the Lord thine oaths. But I say unto you, swear not at all."

Why did He go straightway not to theft, but to false witness, passing over that commandment? Because he that steals, doth upon occasion swear also; but he that knows not either swearing or speaking falsehood, much less will he choose to steal. So that by this He hath overthrown the other sin likewise: since falsehood comes of stealing.

But what means, "Thou shalt perform unto the Lord thine oaths?" It is this, "thou shalt be true in swearing." "But I say unto you, swear not at all."

Next, to lead them farther away from swearing by God, He saith, "Neither by Heaven, for it is God's throne, nor by the earth, for it is the footstool of His feet; nor by Jerusalem, for it is the city of the great King:" still speaking out of the prophetical writings, and signifying Himself not to be opposed to the ancients. This was because they had a custom of swearing by these objects, and he intimates this custom near the end of his Gospel.

But mark, I pray thee, on what ground He magnifies the elements; not from their own nature, but from God's relation to them, such as it had been in condescension declared. For because the tyranny of idolatry was great, that the elements might not be thought worthy of honor for their own sake, He hath assigned this cause, which we have mentioned, which again would pass on to the glory of God. For He neither said, "because Heaven is beautiful and great," nor, "because earth is profitable;" but "because the one is God's throne, the other His footstool;" on every side urging them on towards their Lord.

"Neither by thy head," saith He, "because thou canst not make one hair white or black."

Here again, not as wondering at man, hath He withdrawn him from swearing by his head (for so man himself would be worshipped), but as referring the glory to God, and signifying that thou art not master even of thyself, and of course therefore not of the oaths made by thy head. For if no one would give up his own child to another, much more will not God give up His own work to thee. For though it be thy head, yet is it the property of another; and so far from being master thereof, thou shalt not be able to do with it, no not the least thing of all. For He said not, "Thou canst not make one hair grow;" but, "Not so much as change its quality."

"But what," it may be said, "if any one should require an oath, and apply constraint?" Let the fear of God be more powerful than the constraint: since, if thou art to bring forward such excuses, thou wilt keep none of the things which are enjoined.

Yea, for first with respect to thy wife thou wilt

say, "what if she be contentious and extravagant;" and then as to the right eye, "what if I love it, and am quite on fire?" and of the unchaste look, "what then, if I cannot help seeing?" and of our anger against a brother, "what if I be hasty, and not able to govern my tongue?" and in general, all His sayings thou mayest on this wise trample under foot. Yet surely with regard to human laws thou darest not in any case use this allegation, nor say, "what then if this or that be the case," but, willing or unwilling, thou receivest what is written.

And besides, thou wilt never have compulsion to undergo at all. For he that hath hearkened unto those former blessings, and hath framed himself to be such as Christ enjoined, will have no such constraint to endure from any, being held in reverence and veneration by all.

"But let your yea, be yea; and your nay, nay: for that which exceedeth these cometh of the evil one."

What is it then that "exceeds yea" and "nay"? it is the oath, not the perjury. For this latter is quite acknowledged, and no man needs to learn that it is of the evil one; and it is not an excess, but an opposite: whereas an excess means something more, and added over and above: which kind of thing swearing is.

"What then," saith one, "was it of the evil one? and if it was of the evil one, how was it a law?"

Well, this same thing thou wilt say concerning the wife also; how is that now accounted adultery, which was before permitted?

What now may one reply to this? That the precepts then uttered had reference to the weakness of them who were receiving the laws; since also to be worshipped with the vapor of sacrifice is very unworthy of God, just as to lisp is unworthy of a philosopher. That kind of thing accordingly was now laid down to be adultery, and swearing to be of the evil one, now that the principles of virtue have advanced. But if these things had been, from the first, laws of the devil, they would not have attained to so great goodness. Yea, for had those not been forerunners in the first place, these which we now have would not have been so easily received. Do not thou then require their excellency now, when their use is past: but then, when the time was calling for them. Or rather, if thou wilt, even now: yea, for now also is their virtue shown: and most of all for the very cause, by reason of which we find fault with them. For their appearing such now, is the greatest commendation of them. For had they not brought us up well, and made us meet for the reception of the greater precepts, they would not have appeared such.

Therefore as the breast, when it hath fulfilled all its part, and is dismissing the child to the more manly diet, after that appears useless; and the parents who before thought it necessary for the babe, now abuse it with ten thousand mockeries (and many even not content with words of abuse, anoint it also with bitter drugs; that when their words have not power to remove the child's unseasonable propensity towards it, the real things may quench their longing): so also Christ saith, that they are of the evil one, not to indicate that the old law is of the devil, but in order that with most exceeding earnestness He might lead them away from their ancient poverty. And to them He saith these things; but with regard to the Jews, who were insensible and persevered in the same ways, He hath anointed their city all round with the terror of captivity, as with some bitter drug, and made it inaccessible. But since not even this had power to restrain them, but they desired to see it again, running to it, just as a child to the breast, He hid it from them altogether; both pulling it down, and leading away the more part of them far from it: as it is with our cattle; many, by shutting out the calves, in time induce them to forego their old familiar use of the milk.

But if the old law had belonged to the devil, it would not have led people away from idolatry, but rather would have drawn them on and cast them into it; for this did the devil desire. But now we see the opposite effect produced by the old law. And indeed this very thing, the oath, was ordained of old for this cause, that they might not swear by the idols. For "ye shall swear," saith He, "by the true God." They were then no small advantages which the law effected, but rather very great. For that they came unto the "strong meat," was the work of its care.

"What then," it may be said, "is not swearing of the evil one?" Yes, indeed it is altogether of the evil one; that is, now, after so high a rule of self-restraint; but then not so.

"But how," one may say, "should the same thing become at one time good, at another time not good?" Nay, I say the very contrary: how could it help becoming good and not good, while all things are crying aloud, that they are so: the arts, the fruits of the earth, and all things else?

See it, for example, taking place first in our own kind. Thus, to be carried, in the earliest age of life, is good, but afterwards pernicious; to eat food that hath been softened in the mouth, in the first scene of our life, is good, but afterwards it is full of disgust; to be fed upon milk and to fly to the breast, is at first profitable and healthful, but tends afterwards to decay and harm. Seest thou how the same actions, by reason of the times, appear good, and again not so? Yea, and to wear the robe of a child is well as long as you are a boy, but contrariwise, when you are become a man, it is disgraceful. Wouldest thou learn of the contrary case too, how to the child again the things of the man are unsuited? Give the boy a man's robe, and great will be the laughter; and greater the danger, he being often upset in walking after that fashion. Allow him to handle public affairs, and to traffic, and sow, and reap, and great again will be the laughter.

And why do I mention these things? when killing, which among all is acknowledged to be an invention of the evil one, killing, I say, having found its proper occasion, caused Phinehas, who committed it, to be honored with the priesthood. For that killing is a work of him whom I just now mentioned, hear what Christ saith; "Ye will do the works of your Father; he was a manslayer from the beginning." But Phinehas became a manslayer, and "it was counted unto him" (so He speaks) "for righteousness:" and Abraham again on becoming not a man-slayer only, but (which was far worse) the slayer of his child, won more and more approbation. And Peter too wrought a twofold slaughter, nevertheless what he did was of the Spirit.

Let us not then examine simply the acts, but the season too, and the causes, and the mind, and the difference of persons, and whatsoever else may accompany them, these let us search out with all exactness: for there is no arriving at the truth otherwise.

And let us be diligent, if we would attain unto the kingdom, to show forth something more than the old commandments; since we cannot otherwise lay hold of the things of Heaven. For if we arrive but at the same measure, that of the ancients, we shall stand without that threshold; for "except your righteousness shall exceed the righteousness of the Scribes and Pharisees, ye cannot enter into the kingdom of Heaven."

6. Yet, although so heavy a threat is set down, there are some who so far from over-passing this righteousness, even come short of it; so far from shunning oaths, they even swear falsely; so far from avoiding an unchaste gaze, they even fall into the very act of wickedness. And all the rest of the things which are forbidden, they dare to do, as though past feeling: waiting for one thing only, the day of punishment, and the time when they are to pay the most extreme penalty for their misdoings. And this is the portion of those only who have ended their lives in wickedness. For these have reason to despair, and thenceforth to expect nothing else but punishment; whereas they who are yet here, may have power both to renew the fight and to conquer and be crowned with ease.

Despond not therefore, O man, neither put away thy noble earnestness; for in truth the things are not grievous, which are enjoined. What trouble is it, I pray thee, to shun an oath? What, does it cost any money? Is it sweat and hardship? It is enough to have willed only, and the whole is done.

But if you allege to me thine habit; for this very reason most of all do I say, that thy doing right is easy. For if thou bring thyself to another habit, thou hadst effected all.

Consider, for example, how among the Greeks, in many instances, persons lisping have entirely cured by much practice their halting tongue; while others, who were used to shrug up their shoulders in an unseemly way, and to be continually moving them, by putting a sword over them, have broken themselves of it.

For since you are not persuaded out of the Scriptures, I am compelled to shame you by them that are without. This God also did unto the Jews, when He said, "Go ye forth unto the Isles of Chittim, and send unto Kedar, and know if nations will change their gods; which yet are no gods." And to the brutes likewise He sends us oftentimes, saying on this wise, "Go to the ant, thou sluggard, and emulate her ways:" and "go forth to the bee."

This therefore I also now say unto you; consider the philosophers of the Greeks; and then ye will know of how great punishment we are worthy, who disobey the laws of God: in that they for seemliness before men have taken exceeding pains, and you bestow not the same diligence, no, not for the things of Heaven.

But if thou shouldest reply, "Habit has a wonderful power to beguile even those who are very much in earnest:" this I likewise acknowledge; however, there is another thing which I say with it; that as it is powerful to beguile, so also is it easy to be corrected. For if thou wilt set over thyself at home many to watch thee, such as thy servant, thy wife, thy friend, thou wilt easily break off from the bad habits, being hard pressed and closely restrained by all. If thou succeed in doing this for ten days only, thou wilt after that no longer need any further time, but all will be secured to thee, rooted anew in the firmness of the most excellent habit.

When therefore thou art beginning to correct this, though thou shouldest transgress thy law a first, a second, a third, a twentieth time, do not despair, but rise up again, and resume the same diligence, and thou wilt surely prevail.

For perjury surely is no trifling mischief. If to swear is of the evil one, how great the penalty which false swearing will bring! Did ye give praise to what hath been said? Nay, I want not applause, nor tumults, nor noise. One thing only do I wish, that quietly and intelligently listening, you should do what is said. This is the applause, this the panegyric for me. But if thou praisest what I say, but doest not what thou applaudest, greater is the punishment, more aggravated the accusation: and to us it is shame and ridicule. For the things here present are no dramatic spectacle; neither do ye now sit gazing on actors, that ye may merely applaud. This place is a spiritual school. Wherefore also there is but one thing aimed at, duly to perform the things that have been spoken, and to show forth our obedience by our works. For then only shall we have obtained all. Since as things are, to say the truth, we have fairly given up in despair. For I have not ceased giving these admonitions either to those whom I meet in private, or in discourse with you all in common. Yet I see no advantage at all gained, but you are still clinging to the former rude beginnings, which thing is enough to fill the teacher with weariness.

See, for example, Paul himself, hardly bearing it, because his scholars were delaying a long time in their earlier lessons: "For when for the time," saith he, "ye ought to be teachers, ye have need to be taught again which be the first principles of the oracles of God."

Wherefore we too mourn and lament. And if I see you persisting, I will forbid you for the future to set foot on this sacred threshold, and partake of the immortal mysteries; as we do fornicators and adulterers, and persons charged with murder. Yea, for it is better to offer our accustomed prayers, with two or three, who keep the laws of God, than to sweep together a multitude of trangressors and corrupters of others.

Let me have no rich man, no potentate, puffing at me here, and drawing up his eyebrows; all these things are to me a fable, a shade, a dream. For no one of those who are now rich, will stand up for me there, when I am called to account and accused, as not having thoroughly vindicated the laws of God, with all due earnestness. For this, this ruined even that admirable old man, though in his own life giving no handle for blame; yet for all that, because he overlooked the treading under foot of God's laws, he was chastised with his children, and paid that grievous penalty. And if, where the absolute authority of nature was so great, he who failed to treat his own children with due firmness endured so grievous a punishment; what indulgence shall we have, freed as we are from that dominion, and yet ruining all by flattery?

In order therefore that ye may not destroy both us and your own selves with us, be persuaded, I entreat you; set very many to watch over you, and call you to account, and so free yourselves from the habit of oaths; that going on orderly from thence, ye may both with all facility succeed in attaining unto all other virtue, and may enjoy the good things to come; which God grant that we

may all win, by the grace and love towards man
of our Lord Jesus Christ, to whom be glory and
might now and always, even for ever and ever.

Amen.

---

1. Cf. Nicene and Post-Nicene Fathers: Series I, Volume X:
   Homilies on the Gospel of Saint Matthew / Homily XVII.